THE CLAIRE CHRONICLES

The Claire Chronicles

Published in Nashville, Tennessee, by Elm Hill, an imprint of Thomas Nelson. Elm Hill and Thomas Nelson are registered trademarks of HarperCollins Christian Publishing, Inc.

Elm Hill titles may be purchased in bulk for educational, business, fund-raising, or sales promotional use. For information, please e-mail SpecialMarkets@ ThomasNelson.com.

All Scripture quotations, unless otherwise indicated, are taken from the New International Version˙, NIV˙. Copyright © 1973, 1978, 1984, 2011 by Biblica, Inc.˙ Used by permission of Zondervan. All rights reserved worldwide. www.Zondervan.com. The "NIV" and "New International Version" are trademarks registered in the United States Patent and Trademark Office by Biblica, Inc.˙

Library of Congress Cataloging-in-Publication Data

Library of Congress Control Number: 2018957008

ISBN 978-1-595559333 (Paperback)
ISBN 978-1-595559548 (Hardbound)
ISBN 978-1-595559586 (eBook)

THE CLAIRE CHRONICLES

Trista M. Brazan

ELM HILL

A Division of
HarperCollins Christian Publishing

www.elmhillbooks.com

In memory of my sweet pawpaw Ernest J. Lambert, Jr.
He loved to read, but due to worsening dementia
he was not well enough to know our family's journey.
I am no John Grisham (his favorite),
but I hope this makes him proud!
Pawpaw, may you continue to watch over us in peace from heaven.

Contents

PREFACE

There is a day in my life that has been seared into my memory. I hold on to it although it causes me pain, because it is a constant reminder of my many blessings and my strength. I am quite sure this day won't be the worse day of my life, but for now I can say it is.

On this January day in 2015, I walked through the doors to the cardiovascular intensive care unit to go visit my nine-month-old daughter Claire in Bed 21. She was there in end-stage heart failure from a congenital heart defect (CHD) called hypoplastic left heart syndrome. In the most basic terms, Claire was living with only half of a heart, and the work the surgeons had previously done in two prior open-heart surgeries wasn't enough to allow her to survive. Her only option was a heart transplant.

We weren't allowed to sleep in the CVICU, so I would get there early every morning, and although she was my child it was like I was clocking into work. Claire was so miserable that each day I worked tirelessly to rock her, sing to her, play her favorite shows…anything to make her comfortable and get her to survive just one more day while we waited for her hero heart. On this day, however, it seemed the bottom fell out.

As I walked to her bedside, I quickly glanced at her monitor and saw that her heart rate was already extremely high, in the 180s. I would soon find out that she was running a fever, which elevates the heart rate and respirations. Despite acetaminophen, ice packs, and the oscillating fan, Claire's heart rate kept going up….190…200+, as did her fever. The attending doctor kept coming to her bedside, saying, "This doesn't look good, Mom. This doesn't look good." I swore if he came by and said that one more time without a solution, I would punch him in the face, or at least I would think about it.

I was working with the nurse like crazy to keep Claire comfortable and cool, but to no avail. The doctors then gave the approval for us to give her ibuprofen to help bring her fever down. This was a special exception for a cardiac patient as it could cause additional complications.

About a half hour after the ibuprofen was given it seemed Claire settled down. However, her heart rate was still at about 225 and she was breathing approximately 100 breaths per minute. It almost looked like her chest was vibrating; that's how hard she was working, but she was resting, so the nurse decided to check her temperature again. She looked at me and said, "One hundred and six."

Given the fact that Claire was finally sleeping and that I always learned the word "and" meant a decimal point, I understood her as saying 100.6. In reply I let out a deep breath and said, "Oh…good. That's a relief!"

The nurse looked at me as if I had said the most absurd thing she had ever heard. I'll never forget her expression. "No, 106.1!" she exclaimed.

After that the room exploded with action. The entire medical team descended—more nurses, doctors, respiratory technicians. Everyone shouting orders to each other. They pushed me aside to care for Claire, and I heard orders for a cooling blanket and emergency medicines on standby. Then a different attending doctor came to me nervously and said with a shaky voice, "Mrs. Brazan, I know Claire is a fighter, but I don't see the fight in her any longer. She is tiring out. I feel like we need to do this now."

To which I responded, "Do *what* now?"

"Intubate."

The doctor wanted to put a tube down her windpipe and attach it to a ventilator to breathe for her and allow her to rest. However, in Claire's very critical state intubation could kill her. In fact, I was told that nearly all heart-failure patients who undergo emergency intubation end up in a code with their heart stopping and CPR needing to be administered. Additionally, I had been forewarned that there were no other lifesaving measures that could be done. Therefore if she coded, they would not work on her long before they called her death.

However, I consented, knowing it was her only hope and gave them room to work. The atmosphere in the open ward was electric, but I could sense that everyone was prepared for the worse. EVERYONE, including myself, thought she would die that day. One of the doctors at her bedside caught my eyes and asked me, "Are you staying in here for this?"

"Of course," I responded. "If something is going to happen to my daughter, I am not leaving!"

The nurses attending to the other patients in the CVICU ward came and prayed with me, while also giving me the play by play because where I was standing I could not see all that was happening. I felt a great sense of peace at this moment, knowing that regardless of the outcome God was in control. Either she would live to fight another day or she would go home to her Father in heaven, free of pain and healed.

To everyone's surprise she survived the intubation with flying colors. NEVER expect Claire to do anything, because she will prove you wrong! On this day I was glad she did. Her fever, and subsequently her heart rate and respirations, came down rapidly while on the ventilator and cooling blanket.

Claire would end up receiving her hero heart on March 5, 2015. Though she received this lifesaving gift, she remains a very medically complex child. In addition to being a heart transplant recipient, she also has a genetic disorder known as Turner Syndrome and severe gastrointestinal issues causing her to only tolerate IV nutrition (she eats absolutely nothing by mouth or by feeding tube). Additionally, Claire is also autistic and globally developmentally delayed. Because of these issues Claire has spent the majority of her life in the hospital.

Despite her medical and developmental difficulties, Claire is a happy, content, and beautiful girl. Currently, as this continues to change with age, her favorite activity is to watch *Elmo's World* on the TV and iPad simultaneously while occasionally playing with a variety of puzzles and small objects she can grasp and with which to fidget.

Music is incredibly important to Claire and me. I find she is most content when I am rocking her and singing, which is why all of the chapter titles are song titles. I hope you take the time to look up and listen to some of the songs named in this book. Most have significant meaning, but some titles just fit the theme of the chapter.

The song I labeled "Claire's Song" is the song "For Good" from the Broadway musical *Wicked*. It became her song the night before her first heart surgery, once we heard her grim prognosis. After the consultation with her surgeon, I went straight to the CVICU to hold her and soak up every sight, sound, smell, and feel of my beautiful baby in my arms. I remember singing that song to her over and over that night (and still do to this day), thinking if we would never meet again in this life once she was in the arms of the surgeons, I wanted her to know my entire life changed for good when she was born.

Gone is the naive, easygoing, and dare I say ignorant person I used to be. In her place now stands a strong, powerful, resilient woman poised to defend, protect, nurture, and provide for her family despite the overwhelming obstacles in her way. Because of our family's trials, I have found my strength and the clarity to see the blessings that surround us, even in the midst of many hardships.

Our story is not one of a miraculous healing or an experience in heaven. In fact, you won't get your happy ending wrapped up in a nice package. Some who have read these chronicles have said our story is certainly "interesting and sad but full of hope and positivity." The purpose of this book is to share the lessons we've learned in hopes that they may comfort and inspire…possibly help others. These lessons are not in chronological order; they are simply written in the order that they were placed on my heart to share. The most wonderful aspect of my journey with Claire is my deepened relationship with God. Hopefully this book may help strengthen yours.

CHAPTER 1

SAY SOMETHING

Ever since we found out how medically complex Claire would be and I started sharing our journey with others, people always tell me how extraordinarily strong I am. I mean, don't get me wrong, I am not one to shy away from a compliment, but it tends to bother me a little. I think the reason it bothers me is because I don't feel "extraordinary," and many times I don't feel strong. I am just an ordinary person doing what she has to do to navigate through extraordinary circumstances.

Like many ordinary people, I was not always a very religious person. I was raised in the Catholic church by an A-MAZING mom and have always believed in God. Growing up we attended church faithfully every week; I learned my Bible lessons, and I even sang in the choir. In spite of this I would not say that prayer meant much to me. In fact, when I was younger my typical prayer would have been "please let me do good on this test" or "please let me win the science fair."

Again, in a completely ordinary fashion, as I moved out on my own, I fell out of the habit of going to church. It started when I moved away for college. I did not feel at home in that church community, so I would only attend when I went home to visit my parents. After marriage Kenny and I tried to renew our commitment to church attendance and regular prayer.

However, once again life circumstances got in the way and I fell back to the same old routine of praying only when I needed something.

Before I was pregnant with Claire I was praying because we were having difficulty getting pregnant (again, when I wanted something). Chloe and I would pray every night that "Mom would have a baby in her belly." I remember the day we came home from the doctor with our eight-week ultrasound images and broke the news to Chloe. She ran around the house screaming in excitement, only to come to a screeching halt to say, "MOM, GOD ANSWERED OUR PRAYERS!"

On December 27, 2013, this all began to change. I went to the maternal-fetal medicine doctor as a "precaution" to check the baby's heart because Chloe was born with some very minor heart defects. I was having an absolutely normal pregnancy and everything seemed fine, so I really had no reason to suspect the doctor would find anything. In fact, on the day of the appointment Kenny had the flu, so I asked my mom to come with me. I decided to bring Chloe so Kenny could get some rest, thinking she would think it was cool to see her baby sister, and we'd go out to lunch afterward.

The ultrasound started out pretty normal, and it was fun to watch because we had a nineteen-inch monitor where we could see it live. Then my mom and I could tell something was going very wrong. The ultrasound technician became very silent and focused. She began taking lots of measurements. She excused herself. Then the doctor came in to take some measurements, and then excused herself from the room. Shortly thereafter the doctor came back and solemnly asked me, "Do you want to have this conversation with them in the room?" I looked toward my mom and asked her to take Chloe to the lobby.

By myself, I learned that my precious baby girl had a very complex heart defect and was only protected from it while in the womb. One of the first questions I had was, "Will my baby be born alive?"

The doctor replied, "Yes, more than likely, your baby will be born alive but will need several heroic heart surgeries to stay alive."

I left that appointment without much knowledge of her heart defect, nor was I even in the state of mind even to hear what she had to say. To me she sounded like the teacher from *Peanuts* in my head, "Wah wah wah…" What I did understand was this was different from Chloe's defect. This. Was. Serious…Very.

On the way home, I was struck at how Chloe, at such a young age, understood that something serious had happened. Typically talkative and rambunctious, she stayed silent during the entire forty-five-minute drive home. On the way home the song "Say Something" by A Great Big World came on the radio.

As I sang the chorus aloud, the thought occurred to me that this is how I was feeling toward God. *God, I need you to talk to me right now and tell me why this is happening to me because I am about to give up on you.* In that moment the song turned into a prayer.

When we arrived home I had the awful responsibility of telling Kenny, and the rest of our family, the diagnosis. Once again sensing the gravity of the moment, Chloe scurried off and allowed us to have our time. My parents were there and we all wept together. Then Chloe reappeared. She said, "Mom, I just want to let you know that I talked to God, and God told me to tell you not to worry because everything is going to be okay."

I had begged God during that excruciatingly long car ride home to speak to me, but in His infinite wisdom He knew that I was not truly open to hearing what He had to say. He knew, however, that I would listen to my daughter. She had said, "Mom, it's going to be okay. God's got this!"

Wow. Out of the mouths of babes…

Looking back, this critical moment taught me several things. First, I learned that despite what we want in life we will never be able to control what happens to us. Even in the midst of pain or grief, however, the good news is that God will always be able to bring good out of the darkness.

Second, while you cannot control what happens to you, you can control how you respond. Respond in prayer. When I teach Chloe to pray, I tell her to share three things that she is grateful for that day, one thing she is sorry about, and three things that she would like to ask for, but that prayer does not have to be formal. When I am most overwhelmed I just break it down like I am talking to my daddy. I mean, that *is* what you are doing. Why do we treat God differently? He really just wants you to visit with him and talk to Him, so He can develop a relationship with his child. If you think of it this way and show up for God, He will be there for you—all of the time.

> *"So do not fear, for I am with you; do not be dismayed,*
> *for I am your God. I will strengthen you and help you;*
> *I will uphold you with my righteous right hand."*
> *ISAIAH 41:10*

Like me, you may have been taught to always find a positive in a situation, or if you are struggling through something, to think of all the things for which you are grateful. Being grateful for all God has done for us means being thankful for the tough times, too. I am grateful for this entire journey (which, if you hang with me, you will understand) because it has blessed me abundantly, but those blessings would not have been possible without some truly terrible times.

And when those terrible times come, I know that even though I am an ordinary person my Father is extraordinary, and like Chloe said, "God's got this!"

> *"Do not be anxious about anything, but in every situation,*
> *by prayer and petition, with thanksgiving, present your requests to*
> *God. And the peace of God, which transcends all understanding,*
> *will guard your hearts and your minds in Christ Jesus."*
> *PHILIPPIANS 4:6–7*

CHAPTER 2

BLESSINGS

Coincidences don't exist. This is something I wholeheartedly believe as I reflect on our journey with Claire. The day she was prenatally diagnosed with her complex congenital heart defect, I prayed and pleaded to God to be with me…to help us through this. Little did I know He had already given us one of Claire's biggest blessings, and I was oblivious.

Two weeks prior to her diagnosis, my husband Kenny and I went to our obstetrician for our twenty-week ultrasound. For those not familiar with pregnancies, healthy women usually only receive two ultrasounds—one around eight weeks and another around twenty weeks. The purpose of the ultrasounds is to check on the baby's health and growth, and to predict an accurate due date.

Going into this ultrasound, of course, I wanted to make sure the baby was healthy, but truth be told I was more excited to learn the baby's gender as I had planned a gender-reveal gathering with my family later that night.

When the ultrasound began, it didn't take the doctor long to find our baby. I was immensely relieved to see a beating heart because I had many friends over the years who weren't as fortunate, so I let out a huge sigh of relief. After all, what could be wrong with a beating heart?

The next thing I knew, after watching her little heart beat, I started thinking about my older daughter Chloe, who was born with congenital heart defects. She has three small holes in her heart. The holes are non-threatening and never required treatment. However, in that moment I thought of her, and I asked the question that undoubtedly saved Claire's life, "Can you tell if there is anything wrong with the baby's heart?"

At the time, Claire was so active that our doctor couldn't get a good-enough look at her heart. Therefore, due to our prior history with CHD, he referred us to a maternal fetal medicine doctor for a closer look as a "precaution." Well we now know how that turned out.

I need you all to understand, I NEVER intended to ask any questions of the doctor other than my baby's health and gender. Knowing what I know now, I'd probably have a couple of pages of questions and try to do my best to educate my friends and family on what to ask at their appointments. However, in my sweet ignorance I didn't even know they could detect something so wrong in a baby so small and ALIVE.

<u>5 Heart Questions to Ask at 20 Weeks</u>

Is the heart rate normal?
Do you look at the arteries?
Are the heart and stomach in the correct position?
Do you see four chambers?
Is the heart function normal?

As I mentioned at the beginning of this chapter, it wasn't a coincidence that I thought of Chloe at that moment. That was an act of God. He was already guiding our journey, knowing that with Claire's additional complexities she would not have survived longer than a few days of life had she not been prenatally diagnosed.

Even going back further than that, God knew I needed Chloe in my life first. Much of these stories will center around Claire, but Chloe is my light. She helped ease me into motherhood and makes me look like a good momma with her sweet-mannered exuberance. I call her my light because she is one of the only people who can truly pull me out of my darkness. She is Claire's superhero, because without Chloe…there would be no Claire. I wouldn't have chosen to have another child, nor would I have asked that fateful question that day in the exam room. Chloe was not a coincidence. God knew exactly the plans he had for us and what we needed in order to be ready when those plans were made reality.

In the weeks that followed Claire's diagnosis, we made plans to seek out-of-state delivery and treatment following her birth at a center ranking among the best cardiac centers in the nation. In doing so, we learned that I would have to relocate five hours from home for the indefinite future as the first six months after birth were critical. I remember sitting in our living room with Kenny and my mother-in-law crunching numbers on different housing options, thinking there was no way we could afford this.

At that exact moment I received a phone call from an unknown number. I did what most do with an unknown number and sent it to voice mail. I can't tell you how tired I was of talking to people. When I finally listened to the voicemail, Kenny was worried something had happened to me because I was stunned. Someone I didn't even know, who knew my mom, offered us their rental home seven miles from the hospital where Claire would be born…for FREE. Kenny, the eternal pessimist, thought it was a scam, but I quickly called my mom to confirm she did know the person who had called me. She told me, "Trista, if I were you, I'd hang up and call her back, RIGHT NOW!"

Sure enough we stayed in her home for an initial eight months, both before and after Claire was born and then another six months when we returned for her transplant. What a blessing!

These examples alone happened only in a matter of a month of each other, but over the last four years I could give you numerous occasions of "coincidences" that resulted in countless blessings on our behalf.

So what's the lesson here? Coincidences don't exist. You are meant to be on the path you are on for a reason: that means the good and the bad. If you are on a bad path, please know that I am praying for you; however, remember God is always working in your life for good. If you ask him to show you the way make sure you open your eyes to the "coincidences" that surround you. You will be amazed at his mercies in disguise.

"'For I know the plans I have for you,' declares the Lord,
'plans to prosper you and not to harm you,
plans to give you hope and a future.'"

JEREMIAH 29:11

CHAPTER 3

TRUST

Sometimes I think back on my pregnancy and wonder how my experience, most notably the second half, would have been had I not known about Claire's heart. Even though I let my thoughts wander sometimes, I know it was best that we found out. I had at least three months to make all the necessary preparations for a safe delivery, which gave her the best chance of survival and ultimately saved her life. I will be forever grateful for this blessing. I have known many families who found out about their children's defects after birth, and I have seen the overwhelming whirlwind of activity that consumes them with fear, stress, and anxiety—the same fear, stress, and anxiety I had had several months to process.

Still, I wonder what it would have felt like to be blissfully ignorant of the struggles that awaited all of us upon her birth. How would it have changed my pregnancy? Would I have continued to feel joy when my baby girl wiggled inside me instead of obsessively counting kicks to make sure she was alive? Would I have found excitement in decorating her nursery with a custom color scheme, matching bedding, and accessories all her own? Would I be excited about her birth instead of the feeling of dread, knowing that once she was detached from my body she would fight for every breath she took? What would it have felt like?

After receiving her diagnosis, as anyone would, I, of course, went through a crazy mixture of emotions: fear, anger, heartbreak, anxiety, mourning, etc. Essentially, I was grieving the future I had envisioned for our family and daughter, but above all other emotions I felt peace. It didn't happen right away, though. I had to process what was happening, and WHY it was happening. I knew that no one would come and give me the answers to the latter. However, thanks to my faith-filled family and friends I knew there was a reason, and it wasn't meant to harm us. It was meant to prosper us all. Once I had gotten to the point where I could trust in the Lord's plan, at least what the immediate future would hold, I started to feel that sense of joy, and I made sure others did, too.

First and foremost, I involved Chloe as much as I could. After all, it was Chloe who really prompted us to want another child. We wanted to give her a sibling, and knowing their relationship would be unconventional at best I really wanted Chloe to bond with Claire as soon as she could. Gosh, she was so excited about her little sister, and she loves her so much. Every day Chloe would wake up and come kiss my belly to tell sister and me good morning. She would also get so tickled every time she could feel or see Claire move inside of me.

About one month before my temporary move out of state for Claire's birth, I proposed to my mom and sisters that we should have a baby shower for Claire. My sisters and friends were very supportive of this idea, but my parents were worried. I knew the concern came from fear that Claire wouldn't make it, but I wasn't scared. I knew it was a possibility, sure, but my faith overcame my fear. I didn't want the baby shower for gifts. In fact, there isn't a whole lot of traditional gifts you can give someone in our situation. I wanted to have a baby shower to celebrate. Claire, my precious baby girl, wasn't something to be feared. She was a gift! In her case I always knew that our blessings outnumbered our trials.

Once everyone was on board with the baby shower the plans were set in motion, and my loving family got to work. One afternoon prior to the shower, Chloe saw I was feeling a little down. In typical Chloe fashion (she does not like to see people sad or crying) she fled the scene. She stayed in her playroom for a while, which wasn't all that odd for her. Later that evening she reappeared with a handmade bouquet of paper flowers to lift my spirits. Oh my heart! Aren't I a lucky momma?

Her paper flowers gave me an idea. I immediately called my mom, which I had to do otherwise I would forget, and asked her if she could work with Chloe on the decorations for the shower. You see, Chloe and my mom have a special bond. They share the "craft gene," a gene that must have missed my generation. Nevertheless, these two love to create things together. Actually, I am fairly certain Chloe learned how to make those flowers from my mom. Mom loved the idea, and I thought it was the perfect way to get Chloe involved and make her feel special during the shower.

On the day of the shower, as the guests arrived, you could tell there was a sense of awkwardness in the room. I didn't blame anyone. One of my greatest gifts has always been empathy, to be able to understand what others are feeling and why they feel that way. I can understand how attending an event for a child who may die before she is born would be unsettling. So I made sure to visit and share my sense of peace and joy with everyone who came. After opening the gifts, which largely consisted of baby blankets, socks, hair accessories, and money (there is not much a baby who would spend her indefinite future in the hospital really needs), I gave a nice speech to thank all those who helped plan and those who attended the event to celebrate my sweet Claire. Lastly, I thanked Chloe for always being the light in my darkness and for sharing her faith with me when she could tell mine was lacking.

During this moment in my life, the preparation of Claire's birth, I became very aware of how the enemy could manifest himself in me. The enemy will attempt to use any personal struggle to pull you away from God and bring you down. I am so fortunate I understood this and chose the light over the dark, the joy instead of the grief. I could have let the enemy consume me with fear and anger. It would have been easy to do. In fact, I have let that happen since her birth, and I can tell you it doesn't solve anything. All it does is steal your joy.

In hindsight, I'm glad I placed my trust in God's promises for me. I didn't dwell on the fact that I couldn't decorate her nursery or make some of the normal preparations that expecting mothers do. Had I done that, I would have missed the joy of celebrating this miracle growing inside of me and the opportunity of sharing how God was working in our lives. More importantly, I would have also missed witnessing the bonds of sisterhood already forming.

"A happy heart makes the face cheerful,
but heartache crushes the spirit."
PROVERBS 15:13

CHAPTER 4

LOOK FOR THE HELPERS

Claire loves her PBS Kids television shows. She is so fixated on *Elmo's World* that she watches it all of her waking hours while only occasionally playing with other toys. One of the other little shows that she watches is *Daniel Tiger's Neighborhood*. I think it's actually a takeoff on *Mr. Rodger's Neighborhood*, but I digress.

Anyway, there is always a lesson to be learned from each show and a little "jingle" that they sing over and over to drive home the lesson. In one episode, the child characters are scared because a large storm came through and knocked down a lot of things. The adult characters teach them that when bad things happen they shouldn't focus on those things, but should "look for the helpers." (I'm literally singing the jingle as I type this.)

This particular lesson is poignant in our journey with Claire. You see, prior to being a stay-at-home medical momma I was a nonprofit and fundraising executive professional and volunteer. I spent day in and day out raising money to improve our local community, to help those in need, and put an end to cancer. One of the projects I was particularly proud of was raising funding and helping start a program that assisted over 1,500 families rebuild their homes after flooding from Hurricane Isaac in 2012.

My career truly fulfilled in me the need to make an impact on others, to be a helper.

Kenny on the other hand is quite a bit different from me. He is very family-oriented. He is a fantastic husband and father. (Although he terrorizes the kids for fun. It's his love language, but Chloe wishes it weren't, and Claire couldn't care less.) However, I would never have said he was very generous of his time or money when it came to those outside his family.

Sometimes I felt a disconnect, as if he didn't understand the work I did or why I volunteered so much. I often told my coworkers that I wished something would happen to open Kenny's eyes to the needs of others around him. Well, be careful what you wish.

As you have gathered by now, the news about Claire's health rocked us to the core, and almost immediately we were faced with mounting medical bills. Very early on after her diagnosis, I remember trying to set up doctors' appointments and getting insurance approvals. I couldn't finish the calls without crying uncontrollably because of insurance issues and the out-of-pocket costs that were required. At our very first appointment where we chose for Claire to be born, we were asked to pay $2,000 just to conduct a fetal echocardiogram (an ultrasound of the baby's heart), a procedure that would be conducted countless times before her birth!

It didn't take me long to delegate that task to Kenny because I didn't think the stress was good for the baby or me. I told him, "I promise to take care of the baby and myself and to make sure we make all necessary appointments, but I CANNOT deal with insurance!" Since that day, he handles insurance and hospital bills. Believe me, he has the personality for it.

Additionally, there were a lot of people who kept telling us to seek out the best care for Claire no matter the cost. This was really hard advice to swallow because these people had no idea of what that cost actually was (or is). It's really easy to say to do that, but in practice it took a lot of faith that God would be there to provide for us, and provide He did.

News of our situation had begun to spread throughout our community (perks of living in a small town), and out of the blue people started asking how they could help us or if they could fundraise on our behalf.

Kenny and I didn't know what to think. It was so odd to find ourselves in a position where WE needed help from others. Especially me, since I was always raising money for others. I NEVER imagined needing help, and to the extent we needed it ourselves.

We had a GoFundMe account, football pools, T-shirt sales, dinner sales, a fishing tournament, and more organized for us, and we didn't have to plan or worry about anything. So many people, people I didn't know, friends who I hadn't talked to in over ten years, sacrificed time from other parts of their lives and were coming together to support our family in our time of need. Can you say MIND BLOWN!?

In this moment we really learned a lesson in humility. Instinctively, we wanted to decline out of pride that we could do it ourselves, but in reality we needed the help. Obviously we understood the mountain of bills that were coming in the immediate future, but we also knew that if she survived we would have a lifetime of expenses to bear. We really had to learn to humble ourselves and accept the help others would provide.

Because we have been the recipients of so much generosity, we have truly been blessed to see the best side of humanity. Such a burden was lifted from our shoulders by the help of so many people, many we never met and likely never will. I do believe that people are inherently good and that they seek opportunities to help others. However, I often wonder if we would have received so much generosity had I not been working for years doing the same for others.

I truly believe that we all face consequences, good or bad, of our actions. Ask yourself, what are you doing for others? If you were in need, would others offer to help you? If they did, could you cast your pride aside and humble yourself to allow God to work through others to provide for you?

> "Do not be deceived; God cannot be mocked.
> A man reaps what he sows."
> GALATIANS 6:7

It's not easy to find yourself in need but I believe it is remarkably easy to help others, and there are so many out there who need it. It doesn't have to be monetary. We help people every day through prayer, acts of kindness, or even a smile or a hug when it's needed the most.

After Claire was born we were in the cardiovascular ICU room next to a little baby girl we had been following on Facebook who had issues similar to Claire's. She passed away a few days after Claire arrived, and her mother didn't have enough money to purchase a headstone for her daughter. Kenny, who is not very affectionate, not only hugged this mother in the hallway of the hospital in sympathy but also made a substantial donation to her funeral fund from some of the charity that we'd been blessed with for Claire. In that moment I saw my wish granted. He had become one of the helpers and my heart was beaming with pride. That's my man!

"I know what it is to be in need, and I know what it is to have
plenty. I have learned the secret of being content in any and every
situation, whether well fed or hungry, whether living in plenty or
in want. I can do all this through him who gives me strength.
And my God will meet all your needs
according to the riches of his glory in Christ Jesus."
PHILIPPIANS 4:12–13, 19

CHAPTER 5

GENIE IN A BOTTLE

Lately I have been thinking a lot about miracles. What are they? Who gets them? Are they real? I don't know that I've really figured out what exactly I believe, but here is what I've only begun to work out. I know that I believe God can do anything, but do I feel like if we all prayed constantly for Claire to be completely healed, would she? No, I don't believe she would. I mean, if that's how it worked none of us would ever get off our knees, nor would there be any illness or suffering in the world.

God is not a genie in a bottle: he doesn't grant wishes. Prayer isn't about asking for things you want; it is supposed to be a way to grow in a relationship with God. It took me a long time to realize this because I've been so blessed in my life, but just because you ask for something, it doesn't mean it will happen. Even unanswered prayers can be miracles themselves.

When I think of experiences I would truly consider miraculous in my life, some of them turn out to be things for which I never asked. In fact, I have been in two separate vehicular accidents where I've flipped and totaled my car. In both accidents I walked away with nothing more than a concussion, bruises, and a possible broken nose.

The first accident happened my freshmen year of college. On the way to my on-campus job during holiday break, in morning rush hour traffic,

I fell asleep at the wheel of my car. When I woke up I was looking at the road flying by in front of me. I couldn't see anything else. All I could think was, *Please, God, let me stop! Please let me stop!* I was afraid I would hit someone else or be hit myself. After emergency services came and I arrived at the hospital, the ER nurse asked if I was the one in the accident she passed on the interstate that morning. I nodded, and she said, "Wow! I was sure whoever was in that accident didn't survive. You are very lucky."

The second accident happened four years later and only two miles from my house. I was bundled up for the cold winter day and on my way to work. After being in my car for a couple of minutes, I got warm and decided to take off my scarf. Instead of pulling it off from the side, I dipped my head down and lifted the scarf over my head. In the couple of seconds it took to do that, I had veered off the road and was headed for the ditch. After several episodes of overcorrecting the wheel, I lost control. I skidded across the other lane where the back end of the car hit a small ditch. My car flipped end over end and side over side about five times into the sugarcane fields. I was awake for this accident and just knew I was going to die, but here I am writing this chapter.

About a year after my first accident, a cousin of mine who I loved dearly died in a car accident. As you can imagine, everyone who knew him was devastated. After his passing, I really struggled with the question "Why did I get to survive and he didn't?" The only reason I could come up with is that my story wasn't finished yet, that my work on earth wasn't done. That conclusion always left me wondering what was yet to come. What was I meant to do?

Later I became a very successful nonprofit executive director. My career working and volunteering as a fundraising professional was very fulfilling. I saw firsthand the value and impact my hard work had on those in need throughout our local communities. This feeling always made me think back on my car accidents, and I would think, *THIS is why I am here. God saved me in those accidents to use my gifts to help those who need it the most.*

Then came Claire's diagnosis at the ripe young age of twenty-nine. I never really asked God, "Why me?" or "Why us?" I always knew God had his reasons. However, like most would, I first prayed, "God, let this be a mistake. Let the next time they look be the time they say she is healthy." Never happened. Then "Lord, if it is your will, please heal her and let her be born perfectly healthy." I went to healing services, received the sacrament of the anointing of the sick, prayed to every saint I was supposed to, wrapped blessed prayer ropes around my pregnant belly, said my rosaries…you name it, I did it. It wasn't His will.

This never really made me angry, but it made me stop believing in miracles in the traditional sense. In fact, when people tell me they are praying for her complete healing, it sometimes makes me chuckle. While I know God is very capable, I don't believe she will wake up a normal four-year-old. Additionally, I know too many families, who are probably more faithful than me, who have lost children to defects or illnesses, and I think, *Why should I think I am any more worthy to be granted a miracle than they were?*

I think miracles are all around us, happening every day, and we've all received more miracles to count. God uses his divine intervention to guide us toward our purpose—to bless others or lead others into a closer relationship with Him. I know that has been my personal experience. In speaking with our priest, he reminded me how blessed I am to be so close to God, and that had I not suffered through what we've been through this probably wouldn't be the case.

I can now see that my purpose is to be Claire and Chloe's mother: to have the strength to endure what we've endured and share it with others in hopes that it inspires them and brings them into a closer relationship with God.

"There is a time for everything, and a season for every activity under the heavens: a time to be born and a time to die, a time to plant and a time to uproot, a time to kill and a time to heal, a time to tear down and a time to build, a time to weep and a time to laugh, a time to mourn and a time to dance,

a time to scatter stones and a time to gather them, a time to
embrace and a time to refrain from embracing, a time to search
and a time to give up, a time to keep and a time to throw away,
a time to tear and a time to mend, a time to be silent and a time
to speak, a time to love and a time to hate, a time for war and
a time for peace. What do workers gain from their toil?
I have seen the burden God has laid on the human race.
He has made everything beautiful in its time"

ECCLESIASTES 3:1–11

CHAPTER 6

FRIENDS IN LOW PLACES

"For where two or three gather in my name, there am I with them."
MATTHEW 18:20

Recently, I (finally) had the privilege to attend my first ever "Heart Moms" meeting—after three years of being a heart mom! We got together to relax, love on each other, get makeovers (provided by *moi*) and feel beautiful. When it was over I left with my cup filled. I had so much joy in my heart. It just felt so good to chill with friends who can relate to what I was going through.

Two of the moms I met at the meeting were women who I previously have known only through Facebook (what a crazy time we live in!). For years they have been following our journey, holding us in their hearts, sending me scripture, praying for my family, but until this meeting they had never met me in person.

When I arrived home, I saw a Facebook post from one of the moms: a group picture of us that read, "Friendships born of *literal* heartbreak." In the picture were four ladies who have been through hell, just like I have. Some of them are moms of children who have survived congenital heart defects—like Claire—and some are moms of children who were lost to CHD. So when we say LITERAL heartbreak, we are talking LITERAL.

Although it has been hard, I truly think that I have been tremendously blessed throughout Claire's journey, and this by far is one of the greatest examples of those blessings: the friendships that we have made that would have never occurred otherwise.

When I was at my lowest low, burned to the ground, sitting in the hospital watching my child die, I still met new people, made new friends, shared my story, and helped others. That is God's work.

Many of these first blessings in disguise were relationships with the moms in Claire's "class." In the hospital at the same time as Claire were Aiden, Rowan, and Jackson. Together they were "the summer class of 2014."

I met Aiden's mom Jenny first.

Two weeks after Claire was diagnosed with her heart defect, I got a message from a lady in Shreveport who said, "Oh, my goodness! I just got the same diagnosis. I don't know how I am going to do this. How are you?" This was my first chance to strike up a virtual relationship with a heart mom. We spoke almost every day until we had our babies, two weeks apart, at the same hospital.

By the time Aiden was born I was an "experienced" heart mom. Aiden was brought in for his first surgery earlier than Claire, at just a few days old, because fluid had started backing into his lungs. During the twelve-hour surgery, a physician's assistant would come out with an update every one to two hours. With the first update, Jenny and her husband received some not-so-favorable news of a complication during the first stage of the surgery. Exactly following that update, I walked through the doors of the family waiting room with some warm cookies from a local store. They were obviously upset, but it seemed my visit was just what they needed to lift their spirits and restore their faith. God's timing is always perfect.

Aiden was such a rock star throughout his treatment that he didn't spend even half the time in the hospital as Claire did. It doesn't mean their journey was easier…just different. Even though they were allowed to be discharged, they still had to live within minutes from the hospital in the event of an emergency. So while Claire was in the cardiovascular ICU for "therapy," I would go to Jenny's apartment; we'd eat Papa John's pizza and I would sing sweet Aiden to sleep. Jenny remains to this day one of my dearest friends and biggest cheerleaders. I could not imagine my life without Jenny—a relationship born out of extreme heartbreak.

Rowan's mom Susan also became one of my closest friends. She and Rowan "lived down the hall" from Claire and me in the step-down unit for nearly four months after their first open-heart surgeries. Similar to Claire, Rowan was also living with half of a heart, and while in the hospital together they liked to compete for attention.

In the hospital, kids like Claire and Rowan are continuously monitored. Having lived way too long in the hospital, I actually learned how to program Claire's monitor so it was a split screen of Claire and Rowan's vital signs (heart rate, oxygen level, respirations per minute, etc.). I used the numbers to decide when to visit. After all, I was a good friend and I didn't want to go over there if Rowan was sleeping. Nor did I want to barge in if he had pulled out his NG feeding tube, which happened frequently, and was having it replaced, a fact I could reason from his sky high heart rate.

At night I would watch the monitors and sometimes text Susan to check on Rowan, especially if his vitals seemed odd for him. I would text, *"Claire's saturations are higher than Rowan's! What's going on?"* Again, this was an unusual and text-worthy event because Claire wasn't the top of her "class." The way we saw it, Aidan would go on to graduate valedictorian, Jackson was salutatorian, Rowan would graduate with honors, and Claire would have said, "D's for diploma, y'all. Peace out!" Claire got out by the skin of her teeth. PRAISE GOD!

Susan and I also ate a LOT of chocolate together. We would take turns going to The Chocolate Bar, load up, and share along with some well-stashed wine. (As an aside, there is an ACTUAL place near the hospital called The Chocolate Bar where you can get anything chocolate or chocolate covered. Just a chocolate coated piece of heaven on earth!)

When Claire and I are inpatient, as we often are, I wish my friends were with me, but then I pray that they remain healthy and at home. A hospital is no place to live.

Michelle is another name I will never forget. When Claire was three, she was admitted to the CVICU in septic shock with a very rare bloodstream infection, which only half of those diagnosed will survive. On the fourth night of this admission, after an extremely touch-and-go day, my parents told me that there was a family in the waiting room who had just arrived with their child. Benjamin was a beautiful newborn baby boy with a hypoplastic left heart syndrome. Unlike Claire, he was not prenatally diagnosed and, unlike me, his mom had not had any time to prepare. That night Kenny and I stayed in the CVICU waiting room until the wee morning hours, giving Michelle and her husband the rundown on everything they could expect.

I was also able to reassure her that she was doing everything that she could for her precious baby. Benjamin also ended up at the same hospital that Claire had gone to for a heart transplant. He is doing phenomenally well, and his mom and I are still friends. (He actually received his transplant on my thirty-third birthday!) Looking back, I am still amazed at how God's timing is so perfect. Even in our darkest times God can still use us.

These friends represent just a tiny sampling of the people I have met along our journey who have left an indelible spot on my heart: a reminder of beauty that can come from ashes. Beauty can come from grief.

Don't get me wrong. I have a lot of old friends, too, who are incredibly supportive. What is that old Brownie saying? "Make new friends but keep the old. One is silver and the other's gold." I love all of my friends. The point here is that these are friendships that were forged during what should have been my darkest time. Times when our natural tendency is to close ourselves off from the world and curl up in the fetal position in a corner somewhere. Don't worry, I admit I do feel like that—OFTEN. However, on the occasions of meeting these new people, I'm glad my heart was open to allow these friendships to form because I couldn't imagine my life without them.

At the Heart Moms' meeting there were no pretenses. We were ourselves. We said what we were thinking, and without judgment. If you do not have friends with whom you can be your true, authentic self, find them. If you don't know how to find them pray about it. Maybe you are going through a hard time, and you can't seem to see past your pain. Pray that God will keep your heart open to the possibility that those relationships are there, ready to be forged from *literal* heartbreak.

"He has sent me to…bestow on them a crown of beauty instead of ashes,
the oil of joy instead of mourning, and a garment of praise instead of a
spirit of despair. They will be called oaks of righteousness,
a planting of the Lord for the display of his splendor"
ISAIAH 61:3

CHAPTER 7

A MOMENT LIKE THIS

Life in between Claire's first and second open-heart surgeries was extremely critical. During these four months, patients like Claire were kept under close surveillance in the hospital because things could go very wrong, very fast.

For instance, they had Claire on "cry precautions" because crying for an extended period of time could clot off the shunt that was saving her life. It's so odd because babies cry, that's what they do! However, one day when she was particularly upset you would have thought she was seriously ill. We had at least four or five medical professionals in our room panicking, trying to figure out how to make her stop crying. Then the charge nurse waltzed in, swaddled her tightly, picked her up with both hands like a barbell, and started to bounce her vigorously. That did the trick! Afterward the doctors laughed and said, "This baby needs a bouncer, stat!" It was then we realized she liked to be bounced HARD, a move Kenny and I would coin the "baby bop." I'm an expert baby bopper!

Even knowing her critical state, for us life during this "interstage" period became a monotonous, exhausting series of days and nights monitoring vital signs, medicines, NG tube feedings, pumping breastmilk, doctors, nurses: a rotating door of people in and out all day long.

Claire stayed in the hospital for the first four months of her life, leading up to her second open heart surgery, and for the most part, she was doing pretty well. That started to change in August 2014, when she was three months old. She became really miserable during her feeds. For a couple of weeks Claire would sweat and cry throughout all feeds, often requiring IV acetaminophen, and most times she would vomit her feeds all together.

Because the stomach is the first organ to get cut off from blood supply if the heart function declines, feeding intolerance is one of the first signs of heart failure. They did several echocardiograms of her heart and assured us her heart function had not changed dramatically.

After a brief stay in the cardiovascular ICU, for a reason I don't recall (shame on me!), she returned to the step-down unit a changed kid. She was smiling, and for the first night in weeks she slept well overnight. I remember being particularly upbeat that next day because of the glorious night of sleep I had.

That morning the team rounded, and during their examination they mentioned the word "gallop" several times and ordered another echo to see what her heart function looked like. Not knowing at the time that a "gallop" was not a good heart sound, I didn't think anything of it since she looked so fantastic. The echo was performed, and our day was continuing like all others had before then—meds, feeds, nurses, vitals, etc.

Then the doctors came back…

The staff was like family, so I greeted them with a cheerful, "What's up?" However, that greeting was met with a solemn "not now" head shake. They came to say that even though she looked great, her heart was in very bad shape, "severe heart failure," and that they were admitting her to the CVICU immediately.

Rolling her up to the CVICU, the staff kept saying they never saw a patient admitted to the CVICU who looked so wonderful. We were assured, though, that she was compensating and her heart was, in fact, in end-stage heart failure. They got her started on IV medications to help her heart continue to squeeze, but otherwise we continued our great day in the CVICU with our smiling, happy girl.

The next day things went south rapidly. She was so uncomfortable that no appropriate amount of pain medicine or sedative would help her. Gone was our smiling girl. She had been replaced with a possessed version of herself. (Side note: sometimes when the priest would visit, I would tell him she needed an exorcism. He was not amused.) Next thing we knew they were intubating her and allowing the ventilator to breathe for her so that her heart and body could rest.

News spread to my family that things didn't look good for Claire, and my huge family made the five-hour trip to come visit and, in some cases, meet Claire for the first time.

Once my sisters came into town, things hit me how bad the situation was. The doctors were in discussions about what to do next, but her future looked bleak. While eating lunch with my sisters at the Subway across the street from the hospital, I started to sob at the realization that "yesterday could have been the last day I saw her smile."

I was ANGRY. Do you ever get so angry that you cry? Well that was me. I was angry because I took for granted her amazing day. I just assumed she'd have more, and now I was facing the very real possibility that, while my child was now on life support, I took for granted what could have been her last smiles and baby coos. It was no one's fault but my own because everyone had instilled in me how absolutely critical the time was, but I took it for granted.

She would eventually be taken off the ventilator and would have her second surgery, which helped her recover some function. However, three months later she would be listed for a heart transplant.

It was that day her smile was taken away from me that forever changed the way I look at life. It took that day to teach me to live in the moment. There isn't a moment, a laugh, a milestone for either of my girls I now take for granted. I soak them all in!

However, in the same breath I also admit to getting annoyed with not knowing what's next or what my future holds. The way our life is now, I really cannot plan anything. One of my favorite sayings is, "Want to see God laugh? Tell him your plans." Every. Single. Time. We make plans; we usually end up in the hospital. So while I enjoy living in the moment with my girls, not being able to make any plans for the future because I can't even predict what tomorrow will bring is tough! No lie: I'm still on the struggle bus with this issue.

But then I try to think about it like this: "What if I knew all this was going to happen to me at a younger age?" I would be crushed, and I definitely would never have had any kids! I don't know who I'd be, and maybe I'm giving myself too much credit here, but then I wouldn't be able to live out my purpose to hopefully inspire and help others.

This is precisely the reason God cannot reveal to you your entire future and purpose. You wouldn't be able to handle it. I know I wouldn't.

If we live in the moment, forget the "what-ifs," TRUST God, and be thankful with what we are currently blessed, then we won't have to feel the weight of regret. I'm grateful that God gave me a "warning" lesson and that I have been able to see that big, beautiful smile again.

"Therefore do not worry about tomorrow, for tomorrow will worry about itself. Each day has enough trouble of its own."
MATTHEW 6:34

CHAPTER 8

SHAKE IT OFF

I titled this chapter "Shake It Off" because one of the fondest memories we have of waiting on Claire's transplant is when Claire would dance to the Taylor Swift song "Shake It Off." It was seriously the cutest thing anyone could see. In fact, I would have to teach the nurses how to reset her iPad to play that song and Sesame Street to help keep her calm while we weren't around.

This isn't really the point of the chapter, though; it's about shaking off the haters, which in our case was the cardiologists, intensivists, and surgeons who cared for Claire in her first year. I don't mean any disrespect. I understand their job was to give us the reality of the situation as they saw it, but when it came to Claire there were a lot of STRONG opinions on her prognosis, which was never good. To be fair, now I actually really love all of her doctors and caregivers. However, having to hear how poor her prognosis was over and over again made it so hard to stay positive some days.

When Claire was prenatally diagnosed by a maternal fetal medicine doctor, she made us follow up with a pediatric cardiologist so that he could confirm her diagnosis. When he did, he presented us with our "options." Of course, there was the option to submit her to a life of surgeries, doctors, hospitals, and medicines, or and it seemed in his opinion the better option was to terminate the pregnancy. The latter wasn't even an option for Kenny and me. We would love her no matter how long we would have her.

So now that we had chosen life for our daughter, it was on us to find her the best medical care, which took us to a medical facility five hours away from our home. In the weeks leading up to her birth, we would then find out that Claire also has a genetic disorder called Turner Syndrome. Once this was discovered, her fetal cardiologist sent her "condolences." I didn't understand why we had suddenly left the hope of a 75–80 percent survival rate to now receiving condolences as if there were no hope.

In our meeting with the surgeon prior to her first open-heart surgery, called the Norwood, he explained that children with a genetic abnormality in addition to a complex heart defect do markedly worse than those without genetic issues. He had a very difficult conversation with us, saying that the cardiologists and surgeons had agreed to take her on as a surgical candidate, but her prognosis wasn't good. Even if she were to survive the first surgery, there were no guarantees she'd make it to the next surgery in four months, and if she did, there was little chance of her making it to the final surgery when she was three or four years old. In fact, he specifically said he didn't know of any Turner Syndrome girl who successfully completed the last surgery. Again the decision was ours, and again we were called to life.

As our surgeon predicted, she barely made it to her second open-heart surgery. She was in end-stage heart failure, and the only choice was to move forward with the second surgery, the Glenn, to possibly help reduce the workload of her little heart. He said he wasn't sure she would recover much, if any, function and that most cardiologists didn't think she was worth the risk, but he felt we had come this far so he was willing to try. I remember asking him if there was a possibility of her dying in the operating room. His response surprised me, "Oh, no! We almost always get the patients out alive. If they die, it is typically in recovery." That shocked me because it was very contradictory to what I've watched on *Grey's Anatomy* (one of my favorite but wildly inaccurate TV shows).

Much to my chagrin, our surgeon was nearly always right. She really struggled after her second open-heart surgery. Even at 100 percent oxygen and so much additional life-saving support, her oxygen saturation level was still at only 69 percent. She was so purple. In fact, the anesthesiologist came to me to apologize for bruising her forehead during surgery, saying, "I don't know what I did." It wasn't a bruise at all; it was her red birthmark—some call it an angel kiss or cherry tree—that was just a darker purple than the rest of her little skin. Our newest tagline was "Purple is the new Pink" because we knew she wasn't likely to get any better.

Fortunately for a brief period of time, she did regain some heart function and was able to be discharged home for a period of about six weeks. Then of course came her life flight back for her heart-transplant evaluation. That was such a dark time. The doctors rounded on her every day, and every day I heard how she was likely to die, or that they didn't want to give her more medicines for fear of killing her, or that if her heart stopped they wouldn't work on her for very long.

One day she was so very uncomfortable that every time she screamed, her oxygen saturations plummeted and she would turn purple. The only way to comfort her was for me to hold her, but I could never transfer her back into her crib. After hours of trying to console her, I asked the doctor if he could give any medicine to help her. His response is one that always haunts me. "Mrs. Brazan, Claire is very sick. In fact, she is easily the sickest patient in this unit. Unfortunately, more medicine is not always best. It could cause a chain of events that would be very dangerous for her. We are doing our best not to kill her."

My response is one that I hope he never forgets. "I know good and well how precarious her situation is. I know the risks, but she could kill herself with how extremely agitated she is, and if she is meant to die I would prefer her to be comfortable as she goes."

As you can imagine, it would have been very easy for Kenny and me to give in to such a hopeless and helpless time. I am so thankful for the strength that God continued to give us at the request of so many of our friends and family through prayer. We didn't cave, we fought! We knew that the doctors had to give us the reality, but we knew God had the final say. We trusted in Him knowing that if her story was meant to end, or if she had fulfilled her purpose, God would take her home. But Claire's story isn't over.

> *"Let love and faithfulness never leave you; bind them around your*
> *neck, write them on the tablet of your heart. Then you will win*
> *favor and a good name in the sight of God and man.*
> *Trust in the LORD with all your heart and lean not on your own*
> *understanding; in all your ways submit to him,*
> *and he will make your paths straight."*
> PROVERBS 3:3–6

CHAPTER 9

You Can't Always Get
What You Want

Some people are surprised to find out that just because someone may need an organ transplant, it doesn't mean they automatically get added to the donor waiting list. I know it happens like that on television shows, but that is FAR from reality. My knowledge is truly limited to that of pediatric cardiac transplantations, but the process of getting on the waiting list is a huge undertaking.

On January 8, 2015, around six weeks after being discharged following the recovery of her second open-heart surgery, I anxiously awaited a phone call from Claire's home cardiologist. During an admission to the ICU two weeks prior for a simple cold, it became very apparent that Claire's heart was failing again. That day the plan was to present her case during a weekly conference for all of the cardiologists, including those from her birth hospital, to discuss a plan on how to proceed with Claire's care as the doctors felt they had exhausted all their options, and her last chance was a complicated heart transplant.

On the same day I noticed some strange symptoms. She was extremely irritable. Any time we would start her tube feedings, she was having these dry coughing or gagging episodes, and she wasn't producing any urine.

When I got the phone call from Claire's cardiologist, I was in the vehicle on the way back from the hospital where we had her feeding tube swapped because I thought maybe it was the wrong size, which was leading to the discomfort when her feeds were on, and that perhaps the lack of urine was because we weren't able to feed her much.

Claire's doctor said the team unanimously decided she was in need of a transplant, and they would be sending her back to the hospital where she had had her previous surgeries for an official evaluation. They were planning on electively admitting her to the step-down unit; however, when I mentioned Claire's new symptoms he told us to bring her straight to the ICU because those symptoms were signs of worsening heart failure.

While in the ICU, they started her on some medicines to pull the extra fluid off her organs so they could work better and another medicine to help her heart squeeze. They also arranged for her to be flown immediately to the transplant center. That was Claire's very first plane ride. I was able to fly with Claire, and Kenny made the five-hour drive with our belongings.

We arrived at the transplant center at 3 a.m., but the cardiovascular ICU was abuzz with hectic activity. They immediately ordered a central line for her, and started running labs and looking at her heart with an echocardiogram to determine how bad her heart function truly was. Her test showed what we already knew, she was in end-stage heart failure yet again.

Over the course of the next few days we became familiar with the cardiac transplant evaluation process. For Claire, this would include a lot of blood work and a cardiac catheterization to assess the most accurate status of her anatomy to determine if the transplant would even be successful for her.

Kenny and I had to meet with everyone and "their momma." Well not really, but we were evaluated, as well. We met with the surgical team, the heart failure team, the pharmacists, and psychiatry to see if we were fit to care for a transplant recipient as they require a lot of support.

Most people think organ transplants are cures. As if, "Oh, great, you have a new heart! So you should be good now, right?" Well, no. You are really trading one set of problems for another. First off, in order to keep your transplanted organ healthy you must suppress the immune system so that it doesn't fight the new organ and cause rejection. However, immune-suppression therapy can open someone to all sorts of illnesses that someone with a healthy immune system doesn't have to worry about. Another important point about transplantation that most don't realize is that transplants don't last forever. For cardiac patients, a transplanted heart may last approximately fifteen to twenty years, if you are lucky and don't have any of the common complications like rejection, coronary artery disease, or cancer.

The last point was something that Claire's surgeon specifically wanted to talk about with us. There are a lot of ethical debates on whether organ transplants should even be offered to infants. He did not share his opinion on the matter but just all of the information we should consider. You see, if you give an infant a transplant then at best you are giving her twenty years. So now you have a young adult, at the start of her life who will be critically ill and will need another transplant. If she is fortunate enough to be listed and receive a transplant a second, riskier time, then at best you are extending her life into her forties, which is still young, and a third, even riskier, transplant would be needed. This is a huge contrast to someone who is fifty or sixty who needs a transplant, because that person would have lived a full life and would have a chance to finish out life with family.

Additionally, one must also consider the quality of life for someone so young. At best you are talking about a lifetime of countless medications, lab work, doctor's appointments, and constant infection precautions (just buy stock in sanitizer). In Claire's case the doctors were also particularly concerned about her quality of life due to her genetic disorder, Turner Syndrome.

Claire's genetic disorder coupled with her severe heart defect tremendously reduced her prognosis. They don't completely understand why this is, but the fact is that any child with a complex heart defect and a genetic disorder does markedly worse than a child without a genetic disorder. In fact, one cardiologist referred to Claire as a "ticking time bomb." Can you imagine what they heard from me?

There are only a handful of cases about heart transplantations in girls with Turner Syndrome who were born with Claire's same heart defect. So this left the medical team and us with a big question mark on her quality of life posttransplant. Girls who just have Turner Syndrome and no heart defects are pretty normal developmentally; however, we could already see that Claire was not developmentally normal. Many of us assumed that it was just due to her living in the hospital, but later we would understand that some of it may also have to do with her autism, as well.

Kenny really took what Claire's surgeon said to heart and was so worried about what quality of life she would have. Unfortunately, Kenny often had to be home for work, so a lot of the time when he saw Claire, he saw a little girl living through such misery. Whereas, I had seen glimpses of happier times and thought if we could only help her feel better, everything else would fall into place.

The entire evaluation process took approximately two weeks, and then a medical review board decided whether or not she was a fit candidate to be listed. It is a monumental decision that these medical professionals are faced with because there are so few viable organs (especially for infants) available. They need to be certain that the candidates listed for transplants can survive and thrive with their donor organ.

This was a rough time for us because there were a lot of opinions being shared, a lot of disagreements between the medical staff, and then of course our own inner turmoil. All the while, Claire was suffering. She was so miserable that she would constantly arch off the bed in pain and scream. Sometimes I felt like we were in *The Exorcist*. It was a nightmare. Kenny and I often refer to these times as the "Dark Days of Bed 21."

But on quality of life, Kenny and I discussed it at length. He was very concerned that by allowing her to receive the transplant, we would be extending her misery. I really valued that point of view; however, I just couldn't get over the feeling that this is where we were meant to be. I told

Kenny, "I know your faith isn't as strong as mine, but even you cannot deny that God has guided us this entire way and has made it so incredibly easy for us to be here, in this moment. It's not a coincidence that she was prenatally diagnosed, or that we have a top-rated transplant center within driving distance from our home, or that our housing has been taken care of, that we both have bosses who have been incredibly supportive. That's not coincidence—that's God. I don't think her story is over. I think we need to give her this chance."

Even Kenny couldn't deny that I was right, and ultimately the medical review board (after much debate, probably the most debated patient in history) agreed to list her for her heart transplant on January 20, 2015. She was on the waiting list for exactly thirty days, spending some days inactive due to infection, before receiving her hero heart on March 5, 2015.

On that day she hadn't had an exceptionally terrible day but it wasn't great, either. She was sedated and on a ventilator through her tracheostomy (a hole in her windpipe where the ventilator was hooked) to help her breathe since she couldn't breathe over the sedation required to keep her comfortable until her heart came. I sat by her bedside for hours, like I did every day, just staring at the monitors, praying to see some improvements in her vital signs, but I knew she was dying. That day I just needed to get out, so I left earlier than I typically had and drove back to our apartment.

While driving home I was talking to one of my closest friends and fellow heart moms, Jenny. I was sobbing at how bad things were looking and how hard it was just to be there day in and day out, watching her die. There was also a way to look at the donor waiting list online, without specific patient data, of course, and I had interpreted it to mean there were at least six patients waiting for hearts ahead of Claire. I told Jenny that I felt like any time I could get a call that she was gone.

Just as I reached the driveway of our apartment I got a phone call from the hospital. I told Jenny I had to go because it was the hospital calling and the strangest thing happened. She said with a hopeful voice, "Oh, okay! Call me back and tell me what they said!" In the couple of seconds it took me to switch over to the other line, I was taken aback because Jenny was filled with so much hope that it was Claire's heart, but I was filled with so much dread that they were calling me back to the hospital because she had passed away.

When I answered I heard, "Mrs. Brazan, we have been looking for you! We didn't realize you left early. We have good news. We just received an offer for a heart for Claire!"

Claire's life isn't easy. If you would consider all of what she has been through in the last four years, you would see that she has suffered more than most do in an entire lifetime. Thinking about her quality of life as a medically complex, severely autistic, nonverbal, and globally developmentally delayed child, I often wonder what decisions I'd have made If I knew then what I know now. It's a struggle, but I always come to the same conclusion that we made the right decision.

You see, we view Claire's life as compared to our own experiences of what being a child should be, but Claire is different. She doesn't know any other life. To her the hospital is an extension of her home, and the nurses and doctors are family. As long as she has her iPad, Elmo, and not too many people bothering or blocking her television shows, she is happy. She loves to be tickled, and she laughs at the strangest things. Sometimes I often wish I could see the world through her eyes.

Also, and I realize this could change, her mental development has halted at about six to nine months, meaning that she may feel pain or discomfort at the moment it is happening to her, but she recovers quickly and doesn't take long to forget. Just like an infant getting a shot. I think it traumatizes us more than it traumatizes her. Unlike the rest of us, she doesn't have worries, no one can hurt her feelings, she doesn't care what people think of her—she just lives life on her terms.

While we may see a special needs child, God made Claire perfectly suited for her life. She is a fighter, strong and resilient. She has overcome enormous odds and laughed in the face of statistics. (Do you know only 1 percent of Turner Syndrome girls are actually born alive? Kenny calls her our winning lottery ticket!) She also continues to rewrite the rules of medicine as she never does what's expected, but she is ALIVE and despite all she has been through she still SMILES.

"I have told you these things, so that in me you may have peace.
In this world you will have trouble. But take heart!
I have overcome the world."

John 16:33

CHAPTER 10

RUNNING ON EMPTY

Do any of your spouses, significant others, or parents get annoyed when you let the gas in the car run on "E"? Boy, this drives Kenny INSANE! I never really thought about why it makes him go nuts. I just assumed it had something to do with his "type A" personality. However, after having done some research (for this chapter, of course, otherwise I wouldn't need to know), I now understand that running your car on empty can cause issues with the catalytic converter, fuel pump, and let dirt in to your fuel filter. Now there's your random fact for the day. You're welcome!

I do have a point here, though, and that is bad things can happen when you let your car run on empty too long or too frequently. In the same way, we are like that car, and when we run on "E" we can let the bad stuff in and damage us. I know this personally because I have dealt with the trials of our journey with Claire in two very different ways—filled by the Holy Spirit and on fumes. I can tell you one way is a lot more comfortable than the other.

You would think the first year of Claire's life would have been the hardest for me to handle. A new diagnosis, the unknown, two open-heart surgeries, too many near-death experiences to count, a heart transplant, etc. That's a lot to handle in a year! However, that year I never felt more alive—exhausted of course, but I was always in action to do what was necessary to save my daughter's life.

After Claire's diagnosis I was always busy doing something. If I wasn't researching her condition, I was connecting with heart moms in online support groups. If I wasn't researching cardiac centers, I was scheduling appointments. There was so much to prepare for while she grew safely inside me. When she was born the level of involvement increased exponentially. Sometimes I look back on those times, and I don't know how I survived.

Unlike most new moms, I wasn't the person caring for my child. She was in the cardiovascular ICU being cared for by the medical staff, doctors, and nurses who quickly became my family. Other than being a visitor, the only thing I could do to care for her was provide her nutrition through expressing my breastmilk. Later on I found my footing in the medical world by eventually becoming the best advocate and asset to Claire in the world, but in the beginning pumping was all I knew I could do and could control. So I pumped like it was my job, y'all. If I could only do one thing to help her, I was going to give it my all. It was so hard, though, and painful.

After Claire recovered enough from her first surgery, she was discharged from the CVICU to the step-down unit at fifteen days old. Parents could not sleep with their children in the CVICU; however, on the "floor" it was required. So for nearly four months leading up to her second surgery and another month after her second surgery, I called the "floor" my home. During the initial part of our stay we worked with occupational therapy to get Claire to take her milk by bottle because she had only been getting fed through a tube that ran from her nose into her stomach. I had to attempt to feed her by bottle for at least fifteen minutes every three hours, but I also had to pump every three hours even through the night. So what I would do at night was set my alarm clock for a half hour before I knew the nurse would come to wake me to feed her so that I could pump. Then I had to feed her, and inevitably she would puke all her feeds and we'd have to clean her up. Lastly, I had to clean my pump parts and the parts for the specialty bottle we were using. Finally, I got to "try" to sleep (it's not easy to fall asleep in a hospital) for about an hour or two before I had to repeat.

Gosh, just typing that has me exhausted, but let me tell you something. Throughout all of that I was okay. Sure there were hard times, but I never got to empty. Ever since her diagnosis, I never asked God "Why me?" or "Why Claire?" My faith was strong enough to know that no matter the outcome, God would make something good come out of this. The more we struggled, the more I prayed. I also made certain that my focus was on Claire and our family. I had little time for entertainment, but music has always been so important to me. So during that time, I tuned my station to Christian contemporary because I knew that I only needed to consume positivity and hope. Additionally, we have the best support system in our family and friends that anyone could need. I almost always had someone with me, keeping my spirits up, keeping me stocked in chocolate (thanks, y'all), and hugging me when I needed it. So I was good. I was strong. I was FULL!

In stark contrast is 2017. The year started out with so much hope and promise. Throughout 2016, even though Claire was in and out of the hospital often, a lot of those admissions were spent advancing her forward. During that year we were able to stop her twenty-four-hour continuous feeds and feed her more volume only five times a day, which was huge! Even more exciting was that we were able to get her weaned off the ventilator support and had her tracheostomy removed, as well. I remember being so pumped in January of 2017, saying, "Last year Claire survived. This will be the year she THRIVES!"

My hopes for Claire in 2017 were that after receiving an autism diagnosis in January (I know this would be devastating to some, but it wasn't a big shocker. It was pretty obvious to us), we would be able to enroll her in specialized therapy to help her communicate. Also, I was hoping to advance her physical therapy to get her to walk, and lastly, I was excited to start working on oral feeding.

We had been on a roll without a hospital admission for about six months. Then all of that changed in February. Kenny and I were *finally* going on a date, and my parents came over to watch the girls. After we gave the entire rundown of Claire's feeding and medicine schedule and gathered our things to leave, Claire vomited. Even though Claire has a history of feeding intolerance, she hadn't vomited in approximately a year except if she were sick. My parents encouraged us to keep our plans by blowing it off as a one-time event. No luck there.

That night something broke, and Claire has struggled since. For months we were in and out of the hospital, trying to figure out the feeding intolerance, adding acid reducers, changing formula, going back to continuous feeds, etc. All the while she got worse and worse until she was skin and bones. Looking back at pictures, I still cringe and feel guilty that we let it get that bad, but there were no answers to be found.

May 2017 brought on a rare and life-threatening bacterial infection that caused her to go into septic shock and suffer more misery than one could possibly imagine. In an effort not to be too graphic, let's say this: she developed gangrene in some VERY sensitive areas. Once they started treating the infection appropriately and she regained consciousness, we had to give her morphine with every diaper change for pain from the sores the infection caused. We were lucky that she survived and in record time. We only spent one month as inpatient with that; however, the doctors got too anxious because she looked so good and discharged her home dehydrated and on tube feedings. I would have fought that decision but Kenny was anxious to be home, as well.

Three days later in June 2017, she was admitted for feeding intolerance, dehydration, and malnutrition. In the ER, I told her cardiologist that I was not leaving the hospital without central line access. This was a tough decision because a central line is a direct line to her heart. In most cases, the risk of infection is not worth the benefit of being able to draw blood and get medicines into a patient when there were other means to do that. However, after nearly six months of being stuck several times a day, I felt the risks were totally justified. When I made that announcement, the nurses trying unsuccessfully to draw labs and start an IV in her poor, tired veins backed me on this bold statement.

During this hospital admission, the focus was to still try to get her nutrition through her feeding tube. However, every time the pump would start, Claire would start to gag and vomit. To make matters worse, she was losing protein through her urine. Therefore, she wasn't getting it in her diet of IV fluids, and what she did have, she was spilling it in her urine, which caused her to swell. It became painfully obvious to everyone seeing her swollen body that she needed nutrition, fast, and her stomach was no longer an option, so they put the central line in and started IV nutrition called TPN and lipids (which she still exclusively uses to this day).

Later in 2017, after a few more failed attempts of feeding her, we learned that the contractions in her intestines that are supposed to help the food move along the digestive tract are uncoordinated and actually flow backward up into the stomach and sometimes her esophagus. Also, every time Claire's stomach muscles contract it causes her pain, which is why she gags and retches to relieve herself. Finally, the end of the year was marked with a series of admissions for unexplained fevers, chills, and excessive vomiting, for which we still don't have answers.

Does anyone else need a Xanax after reading that? Goodness gracious!

So as you can see, instead of THRIVING in 2017, like I had it perfectly mapped out, Claire was DIVING, and this momma was exhausted. I was running on fumes. I wasn't sleeping, my diet was deplorable, and I was doing anything to keep my mind off what was going on with my life, which included a lot of chocolate, Coke Zero, and binge-watching Netflix. I also withdrew from many of the people I loved because I didn't want to burden them with my problems.

Additionally, there was my crisis of faith. I couldn't make it to church most Sundays, and when I could, I convinced myself I was too tired to go. I prayed but I was so overwhelmed. I didn't know how or what to pray. I ran out of fuel, and instead of filling my tank I let the darkness in. All I wanted to do was sleep, and the only thing that got me out of bed was my responsibilities to my family. Many times, if we were home, after I got Chloe off to school and Claire's nurse arrived, I'd just go back to sleep until I had to go pick up Chloe again.

The sad thing about depression is that once you are there, you cannot see past your own pain, and things that should bring you joy don't. When I think back on 2017, I want to forget it happened, but if you looked at everything that did happen, we had some shining moments. We took our first family vacation to Walt Disney World, Claire started walking with a walker, Chloe turned out to be an amazing swimmer and softball player, my network marketing business grew, and Kenny and I took a vacation to Punta Cana that I earned with my company.

Eventually, Trista got her groove back, or I should say is starting to get her groove back! Not only did I get on the right medications, I think, I learned that I was not meant to carry these burdens by myself. Did I mention I have some rock star supporters? Talking with my family and friends really helped me, and we came up with a plan to pull me out of my funk. Some of these plans included writing these *Chronicles*, journaling, being mindful of the types of movies I watch and music I listen to, finding opportunities to sing when I can, and most importantly recommitting myself to church and prayer.

I don't have it all figured out, and I doubt I ever truly will, but I can tell you that I will do my best to keep my tank filled. Not literally, though, because Kenny still fusses at me for leaving the car on "E."

"A cheerful heart is good medicine,
but a crushed spirit dries up the bones."
Proverbs 17:22

CHAPTER 11

THERE WILL COME A DAY

Okay, before you go any further, make yourself REALLY comfortable. Get under your favorite snuggly blanket. Grab your favorite beverage. I am about to make you REALLY UNCOMFORTABLE.

Death. Just the word sends chills down your spine, doesn't it? It's such a taboo subject to talk about in mixed company that part of me wonders if I should dare include it in my *Chronicles*. However, the way I see it, I just couldn't leave it out. It's only been looming over our heads for the last four years.

As I am writing this chapter, Chloe is nine years old and Claire three. It is Christmastime, and Chloe recently asked me, "Is Santa a legendary figure? I mean, does he die?"

I thought the question was odd, but I answered her, "No, I suppose he doesn't die."

To which she responded, "I want to be Santa when I grow up so I never have to die."

My immediate response, which I could tell shocked her, was, "Not me, I want to die."

Maybe you are taken aback by my response, too, so let me explain like I explained to her. This world is not made for us. It is hard, unforgiving; full of pain, worry, struggle, etc. However, I believe that when we die, our

Father will be waiting for us, and all of those things will be no more. Our lives of peace will finally begin. Don't you want that, too?

There is no sugarcoating it. Claire's life is HARD. The minute she was born, before I could wrap my loving arms around her, she was stuck with a needle to deliver lifesaving medicines. After watching your child suffer for so long, the belief in a perfect life after death is comforting.

Claire has helped me get comfortable with the uncomfortable things. I have been told more times than I can count that Claire would die from one thing or another. So you may be wondering, if I am so comfortable with death, then why have I fought so hard for her to live?

Believe me, as hard as I have fought for Claire to live—standing toe-to-toe with doctors who told me she was "a ticking time bomb," conducting medical research on the survival rates of Turner Syndrome girls posttransplant to prove her a worthy transplant candidate, monitoring and interpreting vital signs on a daily basis—as hard as I continue to fight, I have also prayed countless times for God to have mercy on her and take her home.

Immediately following Claire's third birthday, after months of being in and out of the hospital because she couldn't tolerate her feeds due to constant vomiting, she developed a serious infection that entered her bloodstream, and she became critically ill. When the medical team got her unconscious body to the ICU, not only did they need blood to accurately diagnose the specific bacteria to treat her infection but also the single IV she had wasn't enough to deliver all the medicines she needed. Because Claire has been poked more times than a pin cushion, the areas for them to give and take blood were very limited. This is not an exaggeration; they worked on her, sticking needles in every extremity she has, nearly nonstop for three days straight, to get the necessary blood and central access for medicines. As a mom, I wanted to yell, scream, and stop them, but I couldn't. We had the best nurses and doctors working on Claire, but her body and her little veins had all been used up.

It was during this hospital admission when I found myself praying for mercy more and more. I would plea, "Lord, if she is not going to make it through this fight, please end her suffering right now and take her home." To me this was the best way I could help her in the most helpless situation.

The fact that she is still here proves to me that she is still living out her purpose. That is why we are here: our purpose. We are the daughters and sons of our God. Our lives are not our own. We are here to fulfill His will. We'll probably never know what it is, a fact that frustrates me more than I care to admit, but I see it every day with Claire. When she isn't doing well, she is calling people to prayer and into a relationship with God. When she smiles, she brings joy to the hearts of everyone who sees it. When she thrives, praises and prayers of thanksgiving are offered up. People continuously tell me how she inspires them daily.

Now death has been thrust in our faces nearly every day with Claire. Kenny and I are realists, and given Claire's history and medical complexities, we strongly suspect we will outlive Claire. However, if there is one thing I've learned about Claire, it's that she always does the unexpected. She may outlive us all! But would I be as comfortable if we were talking about Chloe or another loved one?

The reality is that even though Kenny and I have resigned ourselves to Claire's future, the same future lies ahead of Chloe and all of us. The time frame may be different, but death will happen.

Recently, after some particularly rough months of constantly being admitted to the hospital for reasons the doctors still have yet to figure out (Claire's mission is to rewrite all the rules of medicine, I'm almost certain of it), a fellow heart mom reached out to me. This mom lost her son at three months old to a similar defect as Claire's. I told her I had been wanting to chat with her, but I couldn't bring myself to contact her because I thought if she knew what I'd been thinking about Claire being better off with Jesus, she'd probably want to throat punch me. Her response to me was one of the greatest gifts I've ever received.

"So first of all, I could never hate you or think you're terrible, EVER. You have watched your child suffer miserably for YEARS. My child died before he ever really had the chance to suffer. It's something for which I'm thankful. I've said from the beginning that no matter how much I miss him, love him, and wish he were here, I would never bring him back. I sometimes think I would if he were going to come back with a whole, perfect, healthy body...but then I remember that whole, healthy, and perfect do not exist in this life, on this earth, and then I think it would be extremely selfish of me to take him from heaven where he is perfect and safe. Not that I'd ever be given that chance, of course, but I wouldn't. He is where he belongs, and that's incredibly hard for me to admit because my heart and body still ache for him."

I have experienced a lot of anticipated grief with Claire and couldn't imagine how I'd feel if I outlived either of my daughters. I'm sure there would be a lot of grief, sorrow, and heartache. In any instance of losing a loved one, I hope I can rejoice in the fact that they have fulfilled their purpose and left this imperfect, tumultuous life and joined our Father in heaven for a life of peace and prosperity.

"For our light and momentary troubles are achieving for us an eternal glory that far outweighs them all. So we fix our eyes not on what is seen, but on what is unseen, since what is seen is temporary, but what is unseen is eternal."
2 Corinthian 4: 17-18

CHAPTER 12

TRUE COLORS

As I am sure you are all aware, every month is marked by different "awareness" celebrations. I actually don't mind this too much because it's an opportunity to learn about what others are going through in their lives and to be a little more educated, something that I was oblivious to before Claire.

However, this practice of bringing awareness to issues that our family faces is pretty overwhelming. I never know what group to identify with, and identifying with them all is pretty daunting. Here are a few of the categories Claire falls in:

Turner Syndrome Awareness Month - February - Purple
Congenital Heart Defect Awareness Month - February - Red
Feeding Tube Awareness Month - February - Red heart feeding tube
Autism Awareness Month - April - Blue/multicolored puzzle pieces
Organ Donation Awareness Month - April - Green
Digestive Motility Awareness Month - May - no specified color

Kind of crazy, huh? Claire is one amazing technicolor rainbow of complexities. My sister, who happens to be an amazing pediatrician, recently told me Claire is "one of the most medically complex children she has ever encountered." Not that she was the most difficult to treat or that her prognosis wasn't good, but that there has never been another patient with her combination of medical and behavioral issues. Unfortunately, all of these diagnoses are intertwined, stacking the deck against Miss Claire.

At conception she would have developed a genetic abnormality called Turner Syndrome where she is missing a complete copy of her "X" chromosome. It occurs in one in every 2,000–4,000 girls and only one percent of TS girls are born alive, most being miscarried in the first trimester. The most common features are short stature, infertility, and heart defects. TS girls are expected to be of average intelligence.

Even though Claire's heart defect was detected at twenty weeks of gestation prior to any genetic testing, we know that her TS was the cause of her heart defect. Claire's defect, hypoplastic left heart syndrome (HLHS), is one of eighteen known congenital (existing at birth) heart defects (CHD). CHDs are very common, occurring in 1 in 100 live births; however, Claire's defect is very rare. Leaving her with only half of a functioning heart, the prevalence of HLHS ranges from 1–3 per 10,000 births and is fatal without immediate medical attention within the first few days to weeks of birth.

After her birth, we learned that while children born with HLHS who undergo the series of surgeries to allow the body to function with half a heart had a 70–80 percent survival rate. Claire's prognosis was grim due to her genetic disorder. There isn't an explanation on why this happens, but it is known that children with both genetic disorders and heart defects do markedly worse than children with just heart defects. In Claire's case this was proved very accurate, thus requiring her heart transplant, which was nearly denied because they were unsure of her recovery due to her genetics.

One side effect of heart defects that almost all heart children deal with is some type of feeding issue. The reason for this is because when the heart is not functioning at full capacity, the first organ the body diverts blood from is the stomach so that it can supply other vital organs. Well, Claire couldn't escape this, of course. We tried for about a month to feed her with a bottle, but she never took more than one once and often vomited it. Therefore, she received a gastrostomy tube (directly to her stomach) at one month old. After a near-death experience from choking on thick vomit shortly after receiving her g-tube, they converted her tube to a GJ tube. This tube allows us to put food and medicine past her stomach and directly into her intestines, which should prevent it from being vomited. Claire has an extensive history of feeding intolerance and vomiting, which led us to get a specialized test to see how well food moves through her digestive system (motility). The findings showed that normal stomach contractions cause Claire severe stomach pain and that her intestinal contractions are uncoordinated so that she cannot digest food comfortably. It just swooshes around in her gut. There is no cure for this, and we don't know why it happened. Therefore, now she does not use her stomach or intestines for nutrition. She gets that from a central line where we can infuse nutrition directly into her bloodstream.

Her autism spectrum disorder diagnosis is something that I feel is probably the least related to her other issues. It does add a bit of complexity to her care, though. Most notably she is never able to communicate "where it hurts" or if she is in pain. She is nonverbal, but she does communicate with limited gestures (she knows to bring her iPad to you if it stops), crying and laughing or other content sounds. Her development has come to a halt at around six to nine months, though she is nearly walking. I would also like to add that I don't believe she knows who we are. I think she sees me as someone she likes and finds comfort in; however, she doesn't recognize me as mommy (or Kenny and Chloe as dad and sister), except for when I sing to her. Everyone is the same to Claire—we are all a means to an end. If you can help her get what she wants, which is usually to restart the shows on her iPad, then she loves you. If you won't, then she has no use for you. This often makes my heart ache, but only a little. I am just so pleased that she is happy in her world and not miserable because she can't communicate or is too sick to function. For now that's enough for me. I get my joy in every smile and giggle she gives us.

Because all these issues are rare on their own, combined it makes

Claire's care extremely difficult, just ask any of her doctors. I swear they face-palm themselves anytime they hear that she is in the hospital. On an average week, Claire receives 175 doses of medicine, goes to the clinic for blood work, and attends physical therapy, adapted physical education, occupational therapy, and special education. In an average year she is admitted at least ten to fifteen times. If you can believe it, this is actually all improved from the amount of medicine, equipment, and hospitalization she needed when she was discharged after her transplant.

Despite her issues, Claire is a very content and happy little girl. She is very easy to please as she just loves watching the same episodes of *Elmo's World*, *Super Why*, and *Mickey Mouse Clubhouse* on her iPad. When contemplating a Grant-A-Wish trip recently, I was trying to think of what would make Claire extremely happy. I determined that would only be accomplished by placing her in a room with twenty iPads all playing different episodes of her favorite shows on a continuous loop. Of course, that is not what we chose. I'll keep you all in suspense a little longer to hear where we decided to go.

I often question God, "Why wasn't it enough for her to have a heart defect, or for her to be autistic, or for her to have Turner Syndrome? Why does she have to have them all?" I don't know that I'll ever know the answer, but I do know that in God's eyes she is the picture of perfection. No matter how many mountains we've had to climb, I am grateful for her and all the progress she has made. I truly remember praying for the things we see today. When I look at this sweet girl and see the progress that she makes, despite the deck being stacked against her, I know that she was sent here to inspire us all.

"I praise you because I am fearfully and wonderfully made;
your works are wonderful, I know that full well."
PSALM 139:14

CHAPTER 13

STAND BY YOU

Doctors are smart—well most are, not all. In any event, we come to them with our problems or illnesses and expect solutions. However, there is a reason why medicine is called an "art." There is not always an easy answer or solution to the medical issues people face. As frustrating as it is, oftentimes the appropriate action is to "wait and see."

If you've been unfortunate enough to spend any amount of time in the hospital, especially the ICU, you will quickly learn that the doctors in charge of your care change frequently. Some have weeklong shifts, some are there on the weekends, and some are there just for the day. In the time they have with their patients, they all practice their "art" to help solve their patients' issues, even if they may not completely understand the patients' full medical histories. For patients who are extremely complex or in critical condition, you can see how a lack of consistency may set a patient backward.

While in the hospital, a team of doctors would round on Claire daily to discuss her progress and develop a plan. Like I mentioned, these doctors would rotate frequently. Moreover, when she was an infant it could have been weeks since they had last seen Claire, often when her condition was changing daily. I caught on to this quickly and made sure that I, or someone I appointed, would always be there during every round. It took a little time, but since I practically lived in the hospital I became very fluent in medical terminology. Some people laugh when hearing medical moms speak to each other because it seems we have our own lingo. Now during most admissions, I get asked if I work in the medical field. To that I chuckle and respond, "No, I just live in the hospital."

After Claire was born I became a sponge. I soaked it all up. I knew what every lab value, vital, or alarm meant. I could program the settings on her monitors, take and interpret her vitals, and start/stop infusions, if needed. I often joked that I should be on the payroll, but in all seriousness I was the only constant in her life: the only person in her life who knew everything about her and the only one who knew what was working or what wasn't working. Therefore, I wouldn't leave her side for long.

Every time the doctors rounded I would be right there, front and center. If something was said that I didn't understand, I asked about it. If something was inaccurate, I corrected them. Lastly, if I disagreed with a plan I let them know. I wasn't alone, though. Even though the doctors often changed, we managed to get Claire set up with a list of preferred nurses. This meant only a few nurses would work with Claire, and they knew her very well. They were the ones who typically supported me when I spoke up, especially in the beginning when I was a little intimidated.

I remember my parents visiting at one point. After observing the way I interacted with the doctors during rounds, my stepdad made a comment that I could have been nicer to them. What he hadn't understood was they all wanted to make changes that, in their minds, would move her forward. However, we had already tried some of those things that had made her more miserable, especially as they related to her feedings because of how important it was for her to gain weight. I told my dad, "No, sir. They know that in this room, I'm the boss!"

In stark contrast, though, when Claire's surgeon walked into her room, I wouldn't say much except, "Yes, sir." On the same day, my dad called me out on that, too. He said, "How come you are one way with the other doctors, but with her surgeon it's like you go hide in the corner?" His question really made me think. I came to understand the difference was that her surgeon had had the unfortunate job of telling Kenny and me some of the worst news of our lives. I was terrified of what would come out of his mouth next. It was his decision whether we could move forward or if it would be best to let nature take its course and send Claire home to hospice care. So, yes, I was scared of him. However, when we returned for Claire's transplant evaluation I realized that there wasn't anything worst that he could tell me, and our friendship began. On the day Claire received her hero heart, he happened to be the surgeon on call. When he came to get me to sign her consent form, I said, "I'm glad it's you!"

He responded, "Me, too."

In Claire's case it was so important that I was able to be with her every day. I am positive that we avoided many more setbacks than we encountered because I was able to give the doctors so much valuable information that couldn't be interpreted just from her medical chart. Especially now as she is older and nonverbal, I have to be her voice, her advocate! Lots of people think that the doctors run the show, but the patients and the caregivers are the ones with the power. And if you are uncomfortable with something, you MUST speak up. It could mean the difference in life or death.

For instance, when Claire was undergoing her heart-transplant evaluation, one of the necessary components is a cardiac catheterization to assess the most accurate status of the heart and lung function. A "cath" is a surgical procedure where a doctor goes through a major artery and sends a probe into the heart to measure pressures. In Claire's critical state, this procedure could have killed her simply because she may not have had the strength to wake up from the anesthesia. Because of the high risk, which Kenny and I were aware of, there was a lot of debate among the team of doctors whether the procedure was necessary to decide on her transplant candidacy. She had undergone a cath just five months prior, and many believed the results from that procedure should be sufficient. Others felt that due to her worsening heart failure, her heart function needed to be reevaluated to see if her body could tolerate a transplant. At first I appreciated their thoughtfulness. After a couple of days of deliberation, they decided to proceed with the rest of the evaluation without the cath. She passed all the tests with flying colors. Her case was then presented to the medical review board to make the final determination on adding her to the donor waiting list. When we were told that the review board felt it couldn't make a decision without an updated cath, our immediate response was, "Well, then schedule it!"

Claire was scheduled for her cath the next day. That day, we waited by her bedside, waiting for them to take her into surgery. As the hours passed there seemed to be a lot of confusion because the nurses hadn't heard anything about her case although she should have been taken to surgery already. Later, we were told her case had been canceled because the doctors were still discussing whether or not the procedure was necessary. I swear I looked like the cartoon character with a cherry red face and steam coming out of its ears!

What you need to understand about the donor waiting list is that time matters. The longer you are on the list, the higher priority or ranking you received. The way Kenny and I saw it, they were wasting time. It had been two weeks since Claire had arrived for the evaluation. We knew the cath was a required component of the evaluation and understood the risks. Obviously, if she didn't have to undergo such a risky procedure we didn't want it for her. However, if that was what they needed to get a decision, it needed to happen so she could either be listed or come home and pass away in comfort with her family. And momma bear came out!

I immediately called for a meeting with the heart-failure doctor on service at that time. Later that afternoon, Kenny and I met with her in a private conference room a few steps away from the CVICU. Very simply we told her we were not interested in waiting any longer. Either Claire needed the procedure or she didn't; however, if they felt it was necessary, we wanted it done as soon as possible so as not to steal any more precious time from our family. I'm actually being quite nice here as our words were much more direct and a little crude. We were exhausted, we were frustrated, and our child's life hung in the balance because of their indecisiveness when time was not on our side.

Because we had voiced our concerns, she had her cath the next morning. Not only did she survive the procedure, but also her results were better than expected, and when she was taken off the ventilator, she came out of anesthesia with no issues. She was listed for her transplant a few days later.

I could go on and on with stories where Kenny and I needed to stand our ground to get Claire the care and services she required. I am not exaggerating when I say that there hasn't been a decision made about Claire's care that has not come through me first. In many cases, the doctors will actually ask me what I think we should do. Once they realized I had a thorough understanding of my child's medical issues, we developed a relationship of respect and trust.

I firmly believe God was orchestrating our journey for a long time. Looking back, I can see His hand in everything. I know that not all parents are blessed to have the resources we had to be able to have someone with her at all times, but He knew that our unique daughter would require near-constant attention, and He provided.

Kenny and I both had employers who allowed us to be where we needed to be when we needed to be there without any worry for our income. In fact, looking back to long before we decided to have Claire, I had been so stressed about leaving a very "cushy" job to accept a new position managing local nonprofit, which needed A LOT of work to grow. There was going to be a monetary gain in it for me; however, I wasn't sure the additional income was worth the enormous weight of stress I found myself under. As it would turn out, not only did I help propel this organization forward to increase its visibility and the services it provided to the community, but also this nonprofit provided our family with tremendous support during the first year of Claire's life. My board of directors allowed me to do what I could to work remotely and paid my full salary during that time. I would often tell them how guilty it made me feel to know I wasn't doing a fraction of the work I should be doing, but they wanted me to come back to work for them when I could. Therefore, they told me to consider it a "retainer." Kenny's company also allowed him the flexibility to come and go when he needed and allowed him the ability to work remotely, as well, when he could.

These blessings from our employers, combined with the tremendous support from our community and family, made it situationally easy for me to be with Claire every day. I know this was by design as God knew Claire needed this to survive the challenges with which she was born.

The lessons I gleaned from these experiences and that I wish to relay to you are to trust yourself and know the value of your voice! I've never been a shy person, but I often don't speak up in situations where I am unsure of myself or don't understand what is happening. However, these circumstances concerned one of my most valuable possessions, my child's life! I made sure I learned enough to be a confident advocate for her, because I was not going to blindly trust someone who was meeting her for the first time and wasn't completely invested in her well-being. In these moments I definitely felt my strength.

If something is important to you, don't put it in the hands of those who aren't as passionate as you. Do the work. Get involved. Trust God to give you the strength and understanding you need, and use your voice!

"Speak up for those who cannot speak for themselves,
for the rights of all who are destitute. Speak up and judge fairly;
defend the rights of the poor and needy"
PROVERBS 31:8–9

CHAPTER 14

SHINY HAPPY PEOPLE

Some days I feel like one big, fat liar. As people we have all these different sides to ourselves, some that we disclose and some that remain hidden. Don't get me wrong, I am a very positive, upbeat person—most of the time. However, I struggle with a lot of darkness, depression, anxiety, doubt, guilt, etc.

In my career as a network marketing professional and mentor, I train others that they are their brand and that people do business primarily with THEM, regardless of the products or services they share. It is important to remain positive, to be relatable (not perfect), and to avoid controversy so that you aren't alienating anyone from wanting to do business with you.

That is sound advice, and I do stand behind it. It doesn't serve anyone a whole lot of good to go on a public rampage about something that few care about and that could possibly turn a lot of people "off" from approaching you regarding your product or service.

Because of this, though, I find myself only sharing the good things about myself or the positive things that are happening for our family because I know we are SO blessed. We have two beautiful little girls, and I know there are many families whose situations are so much harder than ours. However, sometimes trying to be one of the "Shiny Happy People" really wears me down, and I am learning it's not good for my soul.

In November 2017, Claire was being admitted weekly for fever greater than 103, chills and vomiting. The doctors would start her on IV antibiotics, rule out a major central line blood infection, and then discharge her with a diagnosis that it was a viral infection, only to readmit her days later.

After the third admission that month, to say I was in a bad place is an understatement. Claire looked like crap: burning with fever up to 105, gagging, and vomiting bile all day and night, and no one could tell us why. She wasn't in heart failure, her labs were looking fine, and no bacteria grew on the cultures. We were starting to explore the option of traveling back to her original hospital, five hours away from home, to get a second opinion. This was a highly stressful decision because there were no guarantees they would have anything different to offer, and we would be splitting up our family for potentially nothing and for no telling how long.

Mostly, I started struggling with the fact that I literally didn't know what was coming next. I have become the most unreliable person I know, which is not me, only due to my circumstances. I cannot plan anything. Without fail, anytime I scheduled something as simple as a haircut or dentist appointment, we were having to pack up to go to the ER for a hospital admission. My health was starting to decline because I couldn't make the necessary appointments to address joint and dental pain due to Claire's demanding schedule. Of the twelve months in 2017, we were inpatient in the hospital for at least seven months of the year, mostly with no specific diagnosis and no one knowing how to help her. That doesn't even include her frequent trips to her specialists and weekly lab appointments in between hospital stays.

During that last admission my walls came crashing down, and the stress of the last four years just hit me like a freight train. I sobbed nearly all night and day. One morning, after crying myself to sleep, Claire's cardiologist came to check in on her. After examining her, he looked at me and said, "Are you feeling okay?"

My response, with no doubt red, puffy eyes, was, "Yes. Why, do I not look okay?"

He said, "No, I guess you just look tired."

With tears in my eyes, I told him, "Truth be told, I would be lying to you if I said this life wasn't taking a toll on me. Y'all should really have a psychiatrist on staff for the parents."

With concern in his eyes, he laughed a little and said, "You're right! It's not the first time we've thought about that. What you guys go through isn't easy. We often wonder what medicines you are on that keep you so positive and perky all the time."

After breaking down to several friends and sharing my struggles with those who follow our journey with Claire, I learned that it is okay to NOT BE OKAY—to not be one of the "shiny happy people." My friends and family didn't turn away from me during these times; instead they lifted me up, validated my feelings, and loved me harder.

"Praise be to the God and Father of our Lord Jesus Christ,
the Father of compassion and the God of all comfort,
who comforts us in all our troubles, so that we can comfort those
in any trouble with the comfort we ourselves receive from God."

2 CORINTHIANS 1:3–4

Believe me, I am still working on this because I am a perfectionist, and I guess I still want to be known for my positivity and kindness, and not the train wreck I feel like sometimes. What I've learned, though, as I begin to share my whole self—the good and the bad—with others is that people connect with you through your imperfections. Truth is, we are all on this earth together, which means no matter how perfect someone looks on the outside, we ALL have struggles and have been given a cross to bear. Perfect doesn't exist in this life.

In the world of social media, everyone is used to seeing the "highlight reels" of people's lives. I think it is really helpful for us to know we aren't alone in our struggles. So many people have reached out to me after I disclosed my struggle with depression because they had been struggling, too, and didn't have anyone to talk to of their troubles. That proved to me that I am not struggling in vain and perhaps my trials can help me relate and create a positive impact on others.

What a lonely world it would be if we didn't have anyone to turn to in times of despair, but we always do: God, our Father.

When I was younger and I would be particularly sad, usually when a boyfriend broke up with me, I would curl up next to my daddy with a pint (okay, who am I kidding, a gallon) of cookie dough ice cream. He'd put his arm around me as I cried, and I knew I'd be okay.

God is that daddy. We don't have to always bring our perfect prayers to Him. Don't forget His Son, Jesus, lived on this earth and felt the suffering of this life. We know that Jesus' prayers weren't always singing praises when he shouted, "My God, my God, why have you forsaken me?"

Still He is always there, ready to hear from you and is okay with your not being okay. The more you share yourself with Him, the more the depth of your relationship will grow. Just like my daddy on earth, my Father in heaven wraps his arms around me, and I know I'll be okay.

"Humble yourselves, therefore, under God's mighty hand, that he may lift you up in due time. Cast all your anxiety on him because he cares for you."
1 PETER 5:6–7

CHAPTER 15

LITTLE LIGHT

About five and a half years before Claire was born, a light entered my world. Her name is Chloe. I always say God knew what he was doing when he gave me her. I was only twenty-four years old when she was born. Looking back I was still a baby myself, but Chloe made being a mother easy. Once we got passed the postpartum depression and colic, we hit our stride. She has been a smart, happy, easygoing child since.

Kenny and I never intended to have another child after Chloe. In our eyes one child was expensive enough. However, as the years passed, Chloe seemed so bored at home when her cousins weren't around to play with her. Growing up with three sisters (not to mention my half- and step-siblings), I always had someone who played with me. I started to feel that ache for Chloe and convinced Kenny to have another baby.

I don't really remember how Chloe came to know that we were trying for another baby, but she was so excited. She would pray every night for "Momma to get a baby in her belly," and when we told her that I was pregnant, she ran around the house screaming and said, "Momma, God answered our prayers!" Once my belly started to show, she would wake up and kiss it every morning. Even after Claire was born, she'd come and hug and kiss my belly. I had to explain that was no longer fun because there was no baby in there anymore, that's just all chocolate! (This is still an inside joke of ours to this day.)

As I've already described, Chloe was with us when Claire was diagnosed and throughout all of the preparations. For the most part, she was always very positive except she didn't like us crying. Sweet girl was always making me crafts to cheer me up. Nearly every day my girl, who LOVES crafts, gave me paper flowers, handmade jewelry, drawings, etc. Eventually, I had a collection of artwork to take with me when I left to have Claire. After Claire made it to the step-down floor following her first open-heart surgery, Chloe's artwork covered an entire wall of her sister's hospital room.

Even so young, she was always so compassionate and inquisitive. I remember her asking once, "Will my sister die before I meet her?" It broke my heart, and I tried my best to say the doctors didn't think so, but it was up to God.

The day Claire was born, Chloe was so proud. She had her "Big Sister" shirt on proudly and never picked up on any of our fear or anxiety. She knew all along that things would be okay. Faith like a child's is a powerful thing! She met her sister in the cardiovascular ICU and never once flinched at the wires attached to her. I don't even remember her ever questioning anything. To her that was just her sister.

One day, after I visited Claire in the CVICU, I came out to the family waiting room. Claire has a pretty big entourage so we took up almost the entire room. I was talking loudly so everyone could hear about how cute her "fat feet" were. Because Claire has Turner Syndrome, she was born very swollen, and her feet were so swollen that it looked like you could pluck off her toes. When Chloe heard me call Claire's feet fat, she came up to me nearly in tears and said, "Momma! That's not nice! Her feet are not fat!" We all had the biggest belly laugh and then explained that calling a baby fat was a good thing, but only babies.

Being a sibling of a special needs child is pretty tough. So much attention must be given to the other child that the sibling can sometimes feel unimportant or not special. This was always my fear with Chloe. I pray every night that she feels loved even when we haven't given her our best. I am happy that she really doesn't feel resentful or neglected at all. I'll be the first to tell you that Kenny and I are not perfect parents. We fail a lot, but when I look at Chloe I know we must have done something right. Perhaps waiting five years in between children was a good thing.

I had to move away from home for six months after Claire was born and then another six months for her heart transplant. Even now that our hospital is closer to home, I still spend a considerable amount of time away from Chloe. I actually missed her entire year of kindergarten and sometimes say that she is a year behind what she actually is because I missed that entire year of her life. This was all much harder on me than it was for her. For her, it was like vacation traveling to visit us after Claire was born. We wanted her to have good memories so we always had an adventure—the zoo, the aquarium, the Cheesecake Factory!

A lot of her normalcy is attributed to our close-knit family. We actually live down the street from all of Kenny's family. Therefore, his mom and dad watch Chloe a lot. I joke that they can claim her on their income taxes because she practically lives there; moreover, Chloe loves them so much, mostly because they spoil her rotten. With them, though, she is able to not miss a beat if we have to take Claire to the hospital. She is able to go to school and attend all her regularly scheduled activities. My family is a huge help, too; however, they usually mostly help me with Claire. My mom is a nurturer and nurse at heart, so she has never been uncomfortable helping me with Claire's care.

One time, upon being discharged from the ER with Claire, I said aloud, "Oh well, big sister won't be happy with this." The nurse in the room gave me a very perplexed glance like, "Why would she not be happy that her sister is well enough to go home?" I had to explain that Chloe was with her granny and would be upset to know that she had to come home. She would be happy that Claire was well, though.

Even though Claire does not interact with Chloe, Chloe is such an amazing big sister and her biggest cheerleader. She loves to hold Claire (even now at thirty-six pounds), help Claire walk, and build puzzles with

Claire. She is so compassionate and is even a big help with her care. She rarely gets aggravated when we ask her to help restart Claire's iPad or her favorite shows on TV. She is very patient and kind.

Again I don't know how we got so lucky. Claire may be our "winning lottery ticket," but we truly hit the jackpot with Chloe! Below is a little Q&A with Chloe as to what life is like, in her own words. Enjoy!

T: What do you remember about Claire being born?

C: Well, I was really young when Claire was born, so I don't really remember a lot. I just thought she would be like a normal kid. I didn't think such a thing would happen to her like being three and not being able to walk. Well, she can walk using her walker, but like she can't really run around and walk and talk and stuff.

T: How do you feel when you see Claire in the hospital?

C: Sad, because if that was me, and I was in the hospital, I'd be sad. But I think I like her being a baby [she is referring to her mental development] because she doesn't really know what's going on and she can't really worry about it. Like, say you told me, "Chloe, you are going to get a shot in like two weeks." I would get nervous because I would be taking like four shots, and I would be worried. Claire doesn't worry, though. She just takes the shots and is done with it.

T: How do you feel your life is different from other kids your age?

C: Well, one thing is that some of my friends complain about how boring or annoying their little sisters are, but if they are here, they think Claire is so interesting. If they would just stay here and see Claire just lying down here and watching TV all day, it wouldn't be that fun, and they wouldn't have a little sister to play with. My friends' sisters will grow up, and they can play together and stuff, but Claire is four and still can't run around and play with me. I have a sister, but I can't play with her like they can.

T: What is the hardest part about living with Claire?

C: Well, if she was older and she kept bugging me all the time, that would be it, but she's not old and she doesn't do that. So, uh. Well, that she can't play with me, and sometimes I get bored and sometimes y'all have to work with Claire, or if Claire is sick my friends can't come over and play.

T: What is it like when we have to go to the hospital?

C: Well, I'm happy that Granny is here for us so that I don't have to go too far away from home, and I can still go to school and stuff, and like, my cousins are right here so I can play with them.

T: How does it feel being away from me when I'm in the hospital with Claire?

C: I mean, I get to FaceTime you, but I still miss you. *laughs*

T: What is the best part about Claire?

C: That she doesn't bug me every two seconds! And she doesn't annoy me when my friends come over, and that she doesn't break my toys!

T: Do you ever feel embarrassed by Claire?

C: No. Well, like whenever we were in Disney and, um, I was kind of a little embarrassed because no one else had a little baby sister with a wheelchair and so much equipment and stuff. I kind of felt embarrassed, but as the days went on, it got better and better because we were having a good time as a family.

T: What else do you want to say about Claire?

C: That I'm happy to have a little sister no matter what and that I can at least enjoy my time with her while she is here with us right now.

T: How are you a good big sister to Claire?

C: I don't know. That I help y'all out? Oh, and I change her iPad every two seconds, and I have to pick up all of her puzzles. Dad makes me pick up all of her puzzles. *eye roll*

T: What is the funniest thing you've seen Claire do?

C: Um *laughs* Whenever you change her diaper and she runs away from you without her diaper on.

"Love is patient, love is kind. It does not envy, it does not boast,
it is not proud. It does not dishonor others, it is not self-seeking,
it is not easily angered, it keeps no record of wrongs.
Love does not delight in evil but rejoices in the truth.
It always protects, always trusts, always hopes, always perseveres."
1 CORINTHIANS 13:4–7

CHAPTER 16

WHATTA MAN

Let's talk about my husband, shall we? Oh boy, this is going to be interesting! When talking to my friends and family about what I should include in the *Chronicles*, a lot of people wanted to hear from Kenny and get his perspective on our journey and our life. My response every time was, "Me, too!"

Kenny is a pretty introverted person. He only has a few very close friends, and he prefers to stay home. Like most men, he doesn't get very emotional and isn't very verbose. Therefore, I knew there was no way he was going to write this chapter by himself. So with his input on my writing, I hope you can get a sense of who he is, and as a man, what he has gone through these last four years.

Kenny and I met when I was a junior in high school. He is three years older than me, and while attending technical college he worked at a local grocery store with some of my friends. While at a sleepover with some girls from my school, my friend Ginger told me she wanted to introduce me to a guy with whom she worked. She wasn't sure if he was dating anyone, but she felt like we would hit it off. Later that night we all decided to go home and get our swimsuits and go swimming. It was then when Ginger said, "I think Kenny is working tonight. We should go see him!"

Knowing what you know of my husband, can you imagine the scene?

A group of five bubbly teenagers and me all showing up at the grocery store to meet this incredibly shy guy. Poor Kenny, he didn't know what was about to hit him.

Once inside, I saw another friend of mine. He and Ginger chatted, and next thing I knew my friend was on the intercom, saying, "Kenny, customer service to the frozen food aisle. Kenny, customer service to the frozen food aisle." At this point even I was embarrassed. Not long after, here comes a tall, slender guy with dark-brown hair combed and gelled forward. He walked with his head down until he met up with us. Excitedly, Ginger said, "Kenny, this is Trista. Trista, this is Kenny. Kenny, isn't she beautiful?"

He responded, "Uh, yeah she is!" Talk about AWKWARD, but I was hooked. He was the first guy, besides my two fathers, of course, to call me beautiful.

Being the shy person he is, it took a little coaxing from our mutual friends to make him ask me on a date. He eventually did, via AOL Instant Messenger (remember those days?), and the rest is history! I love the story of how Kenny and I met down the frozen food aisle of our local grocery store. We have been together for seventeen years now and married for twelve years.

As you can see, we are about as opposite as a couple can be, but in our case opposites attract. Many times when one of us is starting to break down, the other one is strong, which is a blessing that we have each other to lean on.

One of the things I admire most about Kenny is that he is not influenced by others' opinions of him and is not motivated to do anything just to please someone. I've always been a people pleaser, which makes it easy to be manipulated by peer pressure, and I rarely say no. Not Kenny! If he doesn't want to do something, there isn't anything that anyone could do or say to get him to do it. I must also mention this attribute is probably what frustrates me most about him, too. However, it definitely comes in handy as this stubbornness is the exact reason I delegated the task of dealing with insurance and hospital bills to him!

During our journey with Claire, Kenny's experiences were very different from mine, starting with the day Claire was diagnosed. He missed our doctor's appointment because he was ill with the flu. So he had to learn the information second hand from me. Additionally, because we still had a family to support, he needed to work, which kept him home a lot during Claire's most critical times. That first year was especially hard on him because once he got home, he was always being called back to the hospital because Miss Claire was acting up. Fortunately, his employer has always been very understanding of our family's situation and either gave him the time off or let him work remotely from the hospital until she was considered stable enough for him to return home.

On one memorable occasion, Kenny was in town to visit Claire during the time we were waiting on her transplant. Claire had been moved to a private room in the cardiovascular ICU because she was increasingly more irritable and her health was declining rapidly. They thought it best to give us some privacy, which was appreciated. Claire was being kept very sedated so that she could rest and be strong enough should the time come for her transplant. Also at this time, norovirus (a stomach bug that is highly contagious and usually spreads rapidly in confined places like cruise ships) had invaded the hospital.

On the day Kenny was planning to fly back home, I was miserably ill with the norovirus and told him he'd have to reschedule his flight or call a taxi because I couldn't bring him to the airport. He decided to wait another day. Fortunately, I was feeling much better the next day and was able to get him off to the airport as planned.

Having just been sick and not wanting to spread it to Claire, I decided to stay home and away from the hospital. So I called her nurse to let her know, got an update, and made sure she called me if Claire started to act up. She assured me that Claire's vitals were stable and she was comfortable, but she noticed her breath sounds were different than the day before. (As an aside, the nurse on Claire's service that day worked with Claire often and knew her almost as well as I did. On this day it likely saved her life.) The nurse mentioned she would run it by the doctors and give me a call if they wanted to do anything about it.

About a half hour later, I received a phone call from the attending physician, saying that Claire was in respiratory distress. Essentially, her weak body could not breathe over the amount of sedation required to keep her calm and resting. She was not able to exhale enough carbon dioxide from her body and was becoming very ill. Once again they would need to intubate her so the ventilator could take over her breathing as her body was too weak.

As discussed in previous *Chronicles*, emergently intubating a patient in end-stage heart failure is incredibly risky. She could have died from the procedure, but she would have died without it. The doctor wanted me to come in to the hospital, but I told her why I was staying away. She said, "Okay, Mrs. Brazan, but depending on how things go, I may call you to come in anyway." When I heard the concern in her voice, I definitely sensed her fear that Claire wouldn't survive. So I headed to the hospital.

Remember how earlier that morning I dropped Kenny off to the airport? Well, I called him, and he flew right back. He hadn't even landed for an hour before he was needed back at the hospital. This is how Kenny's experience was. I can only imagine being at home worried sick about your wife and daughter, while caring for your older daughter and not knowing if you are coming or going.

Kenny ended up staying for about a week after that occurred because her medical team and we decided it would be best for her to receive a tracheostomy since she would potentially be on the ventilator for a long time while she waited for her transplant. He stayed about a day or two after her surgery, and then went home again. A few days later, I called him to travel back to the hospital…Claire had a heart!

Now that we are home with Claire, a lot of things are different, but some things remain the same. Both Kenny and I feel like we don't know whether we are coming or going. At any moment, we could be taking her back to the hospital for any number of reasons. About THIS, Kenny shares his feelings. I think this is the hardest thing for Kenny to accept, the uncertainty in a given day.

Otherwise, Kenny handles most things very well. While he continues to work outside of the home, he is still a tremendous help around the house and with Claire's care. His Type A personality makes me feel guilty sometimes. For instance, as a general rule you can administer medicine either an hour before or an hour after they are due. Kenny will often walk into the kitchen right on the hour and say, "Did you give Claire her meds yet?"

To him my usual response is, "No, it's only 6:01!"

Between his thoroughness and my medical knowledge (learned from being immersed in the land of doctors and nurses for over four years), we make one dynamic team. Sometimes, having a special needs child can tear a marriage apart. Don't get me wrong, we don't always like each other, but the love and respect are always there. I feel this journey has made us stronger.

Here in his own words is a Q&A with Mr. Brazan himself:

T: Explain what it was like receiving the news of Claire's diagnosis?

K: I was shocked and not expecting it. After that, the stress and anxiety started to set in because of the fear of the unknown.

T: What do you feel has been the hardest part of your life since Claire was born?

K: The hardest part is that there is always something to worry about. When she is sick, you're obviously worried because she is sick, and when she is doing well, you worry about when she is going to take a turn for the worse and be back in the hospital.

T: What are you most grateful for as it relates to the journey our family has gone through?

K: I'm grateful for the moments to see Claire happy and smiling, which is what you live for as a parent of a special needs child.

T: How did you feel about the outpouring of support and generosity surrounding the care for Claire?

K: I'm grateful for the amount of support from friends, family, and complete strangers. The number of people that Claire's life has reached has been amazing.

T: What is your most memorable experience in the last four years?

K: I think the meetings (evaluation process) about if she would receive a heart transplant were the most memorable. At that time, I did not know what the right decision was.

T: Knowing that our life is not easy, how do you cope with the ups and the downs?

K: Listening to music is, no doubt, the way I cope with the ups and downs.

T: Any advice to families of newly diagnosed special needs children?

K: My advice would be to accept your child for what he or she is. Don't get stuck on what you want them to be. Seeing Claire smile and laugh every day always exceeds my expectations of her.

"Whoever welcomes one of these little children in my name welcomes me; and whoever welcomes me does not welcome me but the one who sent me."
MARK 9:37

CHAPTER 17

MISS INDEPENDENT

A lot of people ask, "How do you do it all? How do you manage to be a wife, medical mother, mom to Chloe, successful entrepreneur... how do you do all what you do and stay sane?"

The answer is "with a lot of help (and medicine...TRUTH!)."

I've always been super independent growing up. I am comfortable working in groups with others, but honestly I prefer to work alone. I catch on quickly to most things and I am pretty decisive. I procrastinate the things I don't enjoy, but overall I am definitely a stickler for time and organization, and I can multitask like a boss.

For the most part, these attributes come in handy juggling Claire's demanding schedule of medicines, therapies, and doctors' appointments, while also getting Chloe where she needs to go. The most difficult adaptation I needed to make was accepting help from others. However, I very quickly learned that I couldn't do this all on my own. As the saying goes, it takes a village!

Our support team is unlike any other. My right hand is my husband Kenny. He is incredibly hardworking; however, unlike I imagine most men being, he is very hands-on helping with Claire and housework. I won't say too much about him because he had his chapter. Plus I don't want it to go to his head! He already thinks he is perfect!

Next would be our families. We are so fortunate to live so close to both of our families that they truly step in at a moment's notice to help with Claire and Chloe. When we have to leave in a hurry to get Claire to the emergency room, we call my mother-in-law first to ask her if Chloe can stay with her. If she cannot watch Chloe then we call my parents. We've never been in the position where someone couldn't help with Chloe, and she loves being with her grandparents anyway. They are much more fun than mom and dad.

Besides Kenny, our day nurse, and myself, my mom is the only other person who is able to care for Claire outside of the hospital. Claire is a lot to handle, and I am so blessed that my mom isn't intimidated to do what it takes to care for Claire. She also moved in with me when we were getting ready for Claire's birth so that I didn't have to be alone hours away from home. She also came back for weeks at a time to help me throughout our first year.

Lastly, we have the most amazing network of family and friends. They have not only kept us covered in prayer daily, but they have also fund-raised, brought meals (thank God, because I don't cook), come to visit us in the hospital, and so much more. These are mostly the people I lean on to lift my spirits when I am starting to get down, and they are really good at it.

Specifically, I have been asked to discuss how we deal with the following situations.

Working

As mentioned, I was a nonprofit executive director up until the time Claire was discharged from the hospital following her heart transplant. However, in preparing to come home it was very apparent that I would not be able to work a traditional job outside of the home. We came home with Claire on the ventilator with oxygen, twenty-four continuous feeds through a GJ tube, and over fifty doses of medicines per day (dosed every three hours even through the night). Claire's care was a full-time job.

Both my organization and I agreed it was time for me to step down. At the time, though, Kenny and I panicked a bit because my income was significant, and we didn't know how we would make this work. Upon discharge, her monthly medicines alone were $500 per month. Thankfully, we were able to apply for medicaid as our secondary insurance, which has been a lifesaver.

About the same time, I started seeing some of my girlfriends posting on Facebook about a makeup line they were selling, and it seemed like all of the work was done online. One of my friends actually earned a cruise that year! I was so impressed that I reached out to them for more information. When I learned that I could do all the work from my phone wherever we were (even the hospital), I was sold. I tried the products to ensure I liked them and hit the ground running.

The first few months were very stressful because I had a lot of support and momentum once I launched. I was on my phone constantly, and it frustrated Kenny because I was always short-tempered. Plus I was neglecting Chloe. I once got so involved that I forgot to pick her up from the bus. Being the sweet girl she is, she didn't make me feel too bad about it, but it tore me up. Now I set LOTS of alarms to remind me to stop and take care of certain things, like getting her off the bus.

When I first started my business we did not have a day nurse, and now we do. She works Mondays through Fridays from 8 a.m. to 4:30 p.m. This helps me conduct a lot of my business during the day so that I am able to spend the evenings with my family. I also learned what were the most important income-producing activities and concentrated on those so that there was no wasted time or energy.

I am now in the top 2 percent of the company, have been recognized three years in a row as a Top 10 Seller, earned three luxury vacations, and coach a team of over 700 ladies every day…and still growing. This business has been such a blessing because it allows me the flexibility to keep my family my first priority while also helping provide for my family's needs. Plus the network of women I have met are unbelievably supportive and love my family as if they were a part of us.

How Do You Make Chloe Feel Special?

This one is hard. I'm fortunate that we had five years to spend with Chloe before Claire was born, and she is such a sweet-natured, independent miss herself. Luckily for us, she was old enough to understand why Claire and I had to move away for a little while so Claire could get better. Other heart families I've encountered definitely struggled with siblings younger than Chloe.

When Claire was born, my sisters were in town, and I delegated the task to them to make Chloe have good memories of her birth. While they did visit us, they also had a lot of fun. We always made Chloe's visits to the hospital special. I remember when we celebrated Claire's first birthday inpatient. Chloe was so happy to be there and help her sister smash her cake and open presents. She's always made things so easy on us.

Now that we are home and our life is so unpredictable, and harder in a lot of ways, it's more of a struggle. There are days when Kenny and I are so worn out by the time that she is raring to go. Nevertheless, I do my best to carve out time while the nurse is here to help her with her homework and chat about her day. At night on the weekends, we usually have movie nights (unless she has a friend over, which has become the norm these days). At the end of the day I pray she knows how much she is truly loved.

How Do You Keep Yourself Organized?

We have a lot of "systems" in place in the house. For instance, Claire's medicines are all pre-drawn up in syringes for the week, and we have a medication list from which we work. Our nurse helps us draw them up and lets me know which medicines need refilling. Then I call the pharmacy and request the refills, and Kenny picks them up on his way home from work. Without systems like this in place, our lives would be chaos. I also keep a pretty organized, color-coded calendar, use a lot of Post-It notes, and set alarms on my phone as reminders for important things.

As for housework, Kenny and I have also fallen into a routine of tasks we each do. Unlike many husbands, Kenny does A LOT around the house, which is a huge help. He would say he does everything, but don't let him fool you. I've never seen him dust the furniture! I won't lie, though, I've totally stopped cooking. Hey, I'm not perfect, and it is NOT something in which I excel! I'm not sure exactly how we stay fed, but we manage.

How Do You Remain So Positive?

I try not to think too far in advance and really try to live in the moment. Years ago I could never have predicted I'd end up where I am now. I don't see any utility in trying to forecast the future. I really do my best to focus on the day or week ahead, and believe me that's plenty enough. It seems the more I try to plan things, the more unhappy I become because usually those plans fall through. Our life is so unpredictable; who knows what will happen in one simple day? However, not a day goes by that I don't thank God for the blessings we have, which most days are as simple as thanking Him for spending one more day happy, healthy, and safe together at home with my two beautiful daughters and husband.

Also, I try to remain realistic. Don't get me wrong, I have hope and faith that God is doing wonderful things with my life, but I guess I set my expectations at a level where I won't be disappointed. One day in 2017, Kenny came home from work, and we were discussing bringing Claire back into the ER, where she had just been discharged days before. He was so angry he yelled, "Do you realize that you will be spending roughly 80 percent of your life in the hospital?"

I responded, "Yes! I'm surprised it has taken you this long to see that, and the sooner you accept it, the easier life will be." I guess you can say that I have truly accepted our life and understand the reality we are facing.

Obviously, I am not always positive. There are dark days, days where I just want to sleep, or curl up in the fetal position and block out the world. In those moments I give myself grace and know that it is okay not to be okay. I take a day or two to wallow in my own self-pity, and then I pick myself up, dust myself off, and get back to work. It's okay to breakdown, just don't unpack and live there.

"The LORD is my strength and my shield; my heart trusts in him,
and he helps me. My heart leaps for joy,
and with my song I praise him."
PSALM 28:7

CHAPTER 18

I OWE MY LIFE TO YOU

O n March 5, 2015, while one family was praising God for the blessing of a perfect heart for their dying child, another family was mourning the death of theirs. These *Chronicles* wouldn't be complete without paying tribute to the precious seven-month-old baby girl who, days after losing her life, breathed life into ours.

Throughout the entire time we were waiting for Claire's hero heart (pictured via echocardiogram on the front cover), there was always a sense of guilt. This was one of those times I struggled with prayer. How do you pray for the call saying your child will get the heart she so desperately needs when that means someone else's child has to die? I spoke about this struggle to a heart mom whose child had been, but was no longer, listed for a transplant. She told me to think of it this way: if the unimaginable happened to Chloe or Claire, wouldn't I want to do whatever I could to save another child's life? Of course my answer was "yes." I've been a registered organ donor long before Claire needed a transplant. I wouldn't even hesitate if I were in a similar situation.

After giving what my friend said some thought, my prayers began to focus on giving Claire comfort and strength while she waited, but more importantly for the family of her future donor. I would pray that they would soak up every ounce of happiness with their precious little one before God called them home.

When we got the call saying that we had received an offer of a heart for Claire (I say "offer" because depending on the circumstances of the donor or the patient needing the organ, offers can be refused, and the organ, it would be offered to the next patient on the list), we were told that one of the biggest concerns was the distance in which they had to travel to retrieve it. It was on the very edge of the border for their region. The transplant team was concerned because the longer the heart stayed outside of the body, the stiffer it would become. However, they felt this was Claire's chance, so they accepted the donation.

In speaking with one of the surgical assistants, we were asking her what information we could know about the donor. The only information that could be released was that she was a seven-month-old female. After one year of the transplant, we would be allowed to send a letter through the organ procurement organization that would contact the donor family. The only way we would know any more information, or if they even read our letter, was if they contacted us (my contact information was included in the letter).

It took me a little longer than a year to finally write the letter. As the doctors predicted, her heart was very stiff after transplant, which caused some complications with fluid balance. She needed both peritoneal dialysis and lots of diuretics to pull fluid off her body so that her heart and lungs could function well. This caused her recovery to go on for quite a while, and I didn't want to report any bad news to the donor family like "thank you for this precious gift, but she is still super sick."

A year and a half after Claire's transplant, she had a cardiac catheterization and biopsy. This is how they accurately measure the heart function and check for rejection. It was after this, her sixth biopsy, that we received a perfect report! Her heart was working like a rock star in her little body. In fact, to this day her heart is the strongest thing about her.

We still haven't heard from our donor family. I understand how difficult the situation is for them. I would love the opportunity to tell them

"THANK YOU" in person and for them to meet our precious Claire and to see and hear her strong heart. Just in case the letter never made it to our donor family, I would like to tell them, "We are so incredibly grateful for the selfless gift of life you gave our little girl in your darkest hour. I pray that the God of peace is with you always until you see your daughter in heaven again." Here is the letter sent to this precious family.

To the Family of Our Hero Heart Donor,

Hi there! I am sorry for the delay of this letter. No words, written or spoken, can adequately express our deepest gratitude to you for your unselfish gift of life in the face of unspeakable tragedy. I struggled to write this because I simply didn't know what to say or how to say it, so please forgive me for fumbling through this.

When I was waiting in the hospital with my daughter, who I was told every day would die, I felt so guilty praying that she would receive a heart. The reason being how that heart would be acquired. I didn't want to pray for another child to die in order for mine to live. Instead I prayed for you. I prayed that you would be able to soak in and cherish every moment of life with your beautiful baby before the unimaginable happened, and that when it did, God would help you find the strength and courage to allow your beautiful baby to breathe new life into others.

Now to give you a little information about our sweet Claire. Claire was born on May 1, 2014. We knew, in advance of her delivery, that she would be born with half a heart (a defect known as Hypoplastic Left Heart Syndrome) and a genetic defect called Turner Syndrome.

Claire underwent two complicated open-heart surgeries and a gastrostomy (g-tube) before she was four months old. In some children, these surgeries drastically improve a child's quality of life and their prognosis. However, Claire's surgeries failed her. That is what prompted her need for a heart transplant.

She was life-flighted to the hospital on January 8, 2015, and put on lifesaving medicines. Eventually, her condition deteriorated to the point of needing life support, and she received a tracheostomy so that a ventilator could breathe for her because her body was too weak.

Claire received her Hero Heart on March 5, 2015. After several months of complications, Claire finally recovered enough to be discharged on July 4, 2015. Since then she has been enjoying life at home with her big sister Chloe (8), her dad, and me.

She recently had a procedure done to accurately measure the function of her Hero Heart, and we are thrilled to report that the news was excellent. The doctors said, "You can not ask a heart to function better than hers is." Honestly, Claire has had her share of ups, downs, and crazy complications, but her heart is the ROCK STAR of her little body and is working so well for her.

Claire is now twenty-six months old and has quite the personality. She is a bit developmentally delayed due to her introduction to life and we suspect autism as well. However, she is so happy now and is growing into a beautiful, sweet little girl. Her favorite things are Elmo, Super Why, and her Beat Belle robot. She also loves bouncing ball with her big sister.

I would love the chance to talk with you and for you to meet our beautiful daughter Claire.

Again, words seem simply inadequate to describe the deep appreciation and gratitude we owe you, your family, and your beautiful angel. My thoughts and prayers are always with you.

With Love,
Trista Brazan

CHAPTER 19

A DREAM IS A WISH
YOUR HEART MAKES

Most young couples dream of having a family, and pray that their kids are safe, healthy, and happy. We may dream of them in school, graduating college, getting married, and having kids of their own.

If you are a mother of a special needs child, your dreams for your child's future change. In our world, you dream of a life where technology and medicine catch up with your child so you can eventually do normal things, even as simple as making memories on a family vacation.

As I am writing this chapter, I am on my way home from Claire's Grant-A-Wish trip, courtesy of our local Louisiana State Troopers—Troop C. We were able to experience a magical vacation to beautiful, snow-covered Park City, Utah. Despite Claire's disabilities, she was able to participate in "normal" activities such as snow tubing, skiing (thanks to the National Abilities Center), dog sledding, and sleigh rides.

It's hard to explain how I *know* Claire enjoyed the vacation because she isn't very expressive, except for when she is watching certain parts of her favorite television shows, and is nonverbal. However, throughout our whole trip (including the flights, which surprised me a lot), she was very content. She tolerated being in a new place, around new people, and experiencing new things with ease. There was a magical sense of comfort that flowed through us while we were all completely out of our element. I do need to pause to brag on the LA State Troop C Grant-A-Wish program. The trip was expertly planned, and they anticipated all of our needs before we even knew them. They helped us navigate the airport with ease, had all our medical supplies shipped in advance, and had a comfortable living area set up fully stocked with all the food and goodies anyone could want. Had it not been for them, it could have definitely been as hectic as most trips are. Come on, you know the kind: the ones where you feel as though you need a vacation from your vacation! Nah, this was completely the opposite. We were at peace and free to enjoy life as a family.

The other way, though, that I know she loved her vacation is because she didn't spike a fever or act up, in the way that only Claire can, at all! I mean, we even had the cardiologists in Salt Lake City prepped for our arrival in Utah. Again, whenever you expect or prepare for Claire to do anything, she usually does the opposite.

As a family we made memories to last a lifetime! This was a trip that would probably never have happened if it weren't for being blessed with Claire. We have experienced many traumatic lows but have also been blessed with so much love and generosity.

Again, being thankful for your blessings truly means being thankful for the "bad times," too. It is through our suffering that our relationship with God can grow and we become truly aware of his presence all around us.

However, on our way back home from our trip we had somewhat of a negative experience. Our first flight was slightly delayed, making us late to board our connecting flight. As we rushed to the gate, there was a huge line awaiting family boarding. When we got to the gate to show them our pre-boarding passes, a lady waiting for family boarding told us, "Ummm, there is a line!"

Our nurse, as calmly as she could, stated, "She has special needs."

To which the lady replied with an eye roll, "Oh, right…special needs!"

As I was getting Claire settled, I was commenting that I couldn't believe people could be so rude. In fact, this wasn't the first time it had happened on our trip, but we didn't let that affect our time together. In an effort to make Claire feel normal and comfortable, her wheelchair looks a lot like a stroller. Her numerous scars from open-heart surgeries, tracheostomy, chest tubes, peritoneal dialysis, her GJ tube, and central lines are mostly covered by her clothes. So at a glance she may not appear disabled just like so many of us who have ailments that aren't always visible, especially at a brief glance.

The eye-roller overheard me discussing the incident on the plane and said, "Well, we didn't know!"

Our nurse politely said, "I understand, but it is very frustrating to have people believe we would skip a line for no reason because you can't see her disability."

I also chimed in, "Yes! In fact, we are actually on our way home from a 'wish' trip." I wanted to drive home how special her needs were. Only children with debilitating or life-threatening illnesses are granted these wishes.

I want to take the opportunity to make this a teachable lesson. Please do not make snap judgments based on such limited information. In fact, do not judge at all. That is not our job; that is for God alone. Our job is to love others and to be loved. You'll never know someone's whole story, and I can tell you with absolute certainty that 100 percent of us are suffering with something in our lives. Choose love always and pray others do, as well.

Once we were in the air, and Claire was sleeping comfortably on my lap, I prayed. In addition to my prayers of thanksgiving and forgiveness, I prayed to the Lord for him to continue to bless her and her family so she never feels the burden of caring for a medically complex, globally delayed, and severely autistic child.

"Therefore, as God's chosen people, holy and dearly loved,
clothe yourselves with compassion, kindness, humility,
gentleness and patience."
Colossians 3:12

FEELIN' STRONGER EVERY DAY

It's been three months since I wrote the last chapter of these *Chronicles*, and it just occurred to me that I've never discussed what an ordinary day is like in the life of Miss Claire. It's pretty hard to describe as it's ever evolving, I guess, as most children are at her age. It's strange to think any part of Claire's development as "normal."

As an infant, the typical experience is usually sleeping, eating, pooping, repeat. I realize the parent's experience is much different, especially for moms. Our days are marked with waking up too early, feeding the baby, possibly expressing more breast milk to get your supply up if you are breast feeding or preparing formula if you aren't, cleaning bottles, diaper changes, comforting your crying child, and trying to sleep when they sleep (if they sleep).

I've already mentioned what a typical day in the hospital was like as an infant for Claire, except for in the CVICU, which is a bit different. Life in the hospital is a never-ending revolving door of medical students, residents, and attending doctors all asking how she did overnight and creating a daily plan of care. Then there are nurses bringing in medicines and taking vitals. In Claire's case, these events were usually every one to three hours. Because I wasn't allowed to breast feed her, I pumped my breast milk every three hours and also had to try (unsuccessfully) to bottle feed her. This would usually also lead to a tubal feed that would usually end in vomit. Not to mention the normal parenting duties of diaper changes and cleaning the pump parts and bottles. Whenever Kenny or my mom were around, I delegated those tasks to them so that I could sleep.

During Claire's most critical time, from about nine to thirteen months old, I would say her days deviated greatly from a normal baby's experience. She was essentially confined to her crib and attached to heart and oxygen monitors, usually some type of respiratory equipment (oxygen or ventilator), and multiple IVs or central lines in her to give medicines to keep her alive and take labs to assess her current health. She would also have numerous ultrasounds or tests to ensure the doctors weren't missing anything due to how miserable she was. We did our best to try to keep her happy with stuffed animals, toys, books, and above all—the almighty iPad. Additionally, to make sure we tried to help her not fall too far behind developmentally, we would try physical and occupational therapy. However, she was usually too uncomfortable to participate.

On our end, depending on if any family was with me, we would get there at around 7 a.m. and stick around her bedside, helping make her as comfortable as we could until the medical team rounded so that we knew what the plan was for the day. Then we would allow family to visit, if she was feeling well enough, while we went and ate some lunch. When family wasn't there I would sit by her bedside praying and focusing on the stupid monitors. I had a real love-hate relationship with those numbers and my day was either made or decimated by what I saw. At some point in the evening, we would leave, eat dinner, go to our apartment, and sleep. Just before I went to bed every night, I would call the night nurse for a report and stress that if anything should happen, I mean anything, I need to be called. I usually never got a call at night. Only a few major events happened at night, and they would usually hear it from me the next day if I hadn't been informed.

When we were discharged posttransplant, after over a year spent in the hospital, life at home was ridiculous. I feel as if I have a mental block of that time because it was relentlessly exhausting. Claire came home from the hospital with a tracheostomy, portable ventilator with oxygen attached, twenty-four-hour continuous tube feedings into her intestines, over thirty medicines that we alternated dosing every three hours (nearly 200 doses per day), and NO nurse. She slept in a toddler bed in our living room, on a padded inclined pillow, which we had a sling attached to that we could strap her into so she couldn't roll over or flip out. Next to her stood a metal cart that held all of her equipment, and fortunately someone custom made a changing table on wheels for us where we could do her daily baths, trach, and GJ-tube care in the living area. When she woke up, she spent the day on a gymnastics mat covered by a blanket where she could have the freedom to lie down and play with her toys. At least once a day we would sit her up in a high chair so that she could sit supported and play with some of her toys upright.

After several months of being home and surviving from day to day, we were finally approved for a private duty nurse to assist us with Claire. Private duty nursing can be extremely helpful or extremely stressful. Many private duty nursing companies do not compensate their employees well enough and don't offer any benefits. Therefore, when Claire is admitted to the hospital, which is A LOT, the nurses either have to pick up another case temporarily, if one is available, or they won't get paid. It is because of this that we lost a lot of great nurses—nurses who made our life so much easier and became a part of our family. I often find myself in what seems like a never-ending cycle of training nurses, which is the extremely stressful part. Some nurses haven't even lasted a whole shift before we moved on to the next, while the good ones leave for one reason or another. On other times, the staffing has been so short that there simply are no nurses available to accommodate us.

While at home Claire has numerous doctor visits and also gets home-based physical, speech, and occupational therapies in addition to special education. While we continue to do a lot of the same things we once have, as she has gotten older and a lot more medically stable, the frequency of her doctor visits has reduced, as has the amount of medicines. PRAISE GOD!

When we took Claire home at fourteen months old, she was unable to sit up on her own and did not really make a whole lot of sounds. Now, although her developmental age is still about six to nine months, she babbles constantly, is communicating with us through some sounds and gestures, and can now stand, crawl, and walk with assistance.

I try to consolidate any doctors' appointments she may have to once a week. She no longer has to get poked as often as she used to because the central line in her chest allows the nurses to attach a syringe and draw back the blood they need. This is not typical for transplant patients. However, Claire has always been atypical. Additionally, her central line continuously provides her with IV-based nutrition for twenty hours a day since we've established that her stomach is just for show. Just kidding! She does use her digestive system for medicine, which is currently down to only NINE! BONUS: we no longer have to wake up or wake her up to give her medicines. HALLELUJAH!

My role with her on a typical day is to wake her up, dress her, change the dressing around her GJ tube, fix her hair, and let her play. Claire's nurse helps us out Mondays through Fridays from 8 a.m. to 4:30 p.m. The nurse takes her vitals, helps keep her safe so she doesn't break her central line, keeps her content by restarting her iPad and television shows, plays with her, gives her medicines, draws up meds, and helps make sure she walks with her walker throughout the day.

Once Kenny gets home and I come out of my office from working my at-home businesses, it's family time. She is able to get disconnected from her continuous infusion for four hours. For those four hours she can roam around the living area and do what she likes within reason. We like to play with her and get her to try new things like taking steps on her own, and she sometimes enjoys being tickled. We hold her and snuggle with her a lot, too. Chloe sometimes gets in on the action, although they don't interact a whole lot. Chloe loves to help her sister walk and tries to make up fun games that Claire "participates" in by coincidence. For instance, sometimes when Claire gets super excited, she makes noises like a monkey. So for amusement during those times, Chloe will say, "Claire, what does the monkey say?" It's really funny when she gets the timing just right. Mostly, Chloe just laughs at her sister because she toots (passes gas) LOUDLY all the time.

As I am currently writing this, Claire is relatively stable, only having been admitted to the hospital twice in the last seven months, and we are preparing for her to start preschool soon. When people ask how she is doing, I hesitate to say she is doing well for fear I will jinx us. We live our lives not knowing how or where we'll end up each day, knowing that her, Chloe, or our health can change in an instant.

My "doctor sister" tells her new parents all the time, "When you become a parent the two most prominent emotions are always FEAR and GUILT." To that I say a big AMEN. I think that is how our lives differ from most: we are able to see so crystal clear how truly fragile life is. It's overwhelming to know that nothing is in our control, but when we have faith in the One who is in control there can be peace. Also, when you believe in a perfect and eternal life after your human life on earth ends, you are released from the chokehold of fear that can suffocate you.

That feeling is my hope for all who read these *Chronicles*. I hope you all can see God's presence in all of the little coincidences in your life and know that you are not alone through any hardships you may face. Trust that the One who holds your future will guide you safely there.

PHOTO SECTION

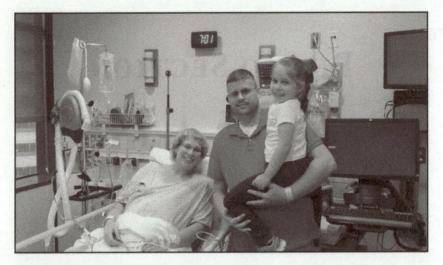

May 1, 2014- Our last picture as a family of three before Claire's birth.

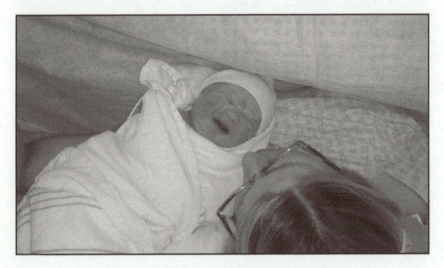

May 1, 2014- Claire Adele Brazan was born with
Hypoplastic Left Heart Syndrome (HLHS) and Turner Syndrome.

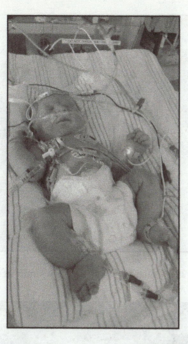

May 2014- Claire awaiting surgery in the cardiovascular ICU.

May 2014- Mom holds Claire for the first time five days after her birth.

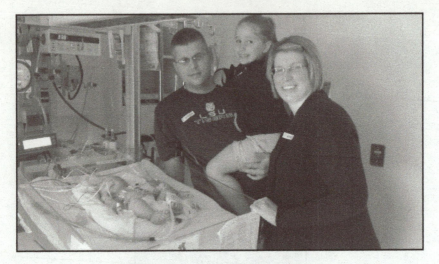

May 2014- First family picture as a family of four.

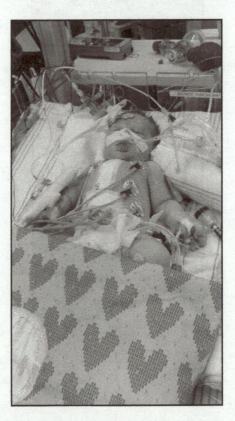

May 10, 2014- Three days post op from her first open-heart surgery (Norwood).

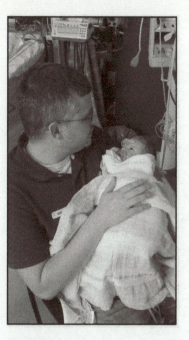

May 2014- Dad finally holds Claire for the first time three weeks after birth.

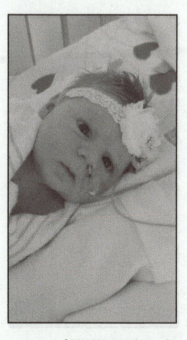

May 2014- Claire moves out of CVICU onto the cardiac step-down floor.

May 2014- One of many drawings big sister, Chloe, drew for her baby sister.

June 2014- Chloe snuggling with little sister, Claire.

August 2014- Despite being in a great mood, we learned Claire was in severe heart failure and required a transfer to the CVICU.

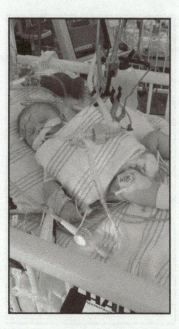

August 2014- Once diagnosed with end-stage heart failure, Claire deteriorated rapidly. She was intubated and sedated to allow her body to rest.

Mom and sister visit Claire to soak up all her smiles before her next open-heart surgery.

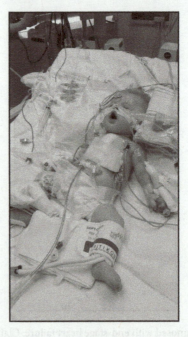

September 2, 2014- Claire receives second open-heart surgery (Glenn).

October 2014- Claire has recovered enough to be discharged from the hospital.

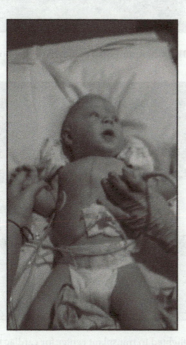

November 2014- Claire's first cardiology visit and echocardiogram home in Louisiana.

December 2014- Chloe and Claire enjoying being home together.

January 8, 2015- Life flighted to transplant center for cardiac transplant evaluation.

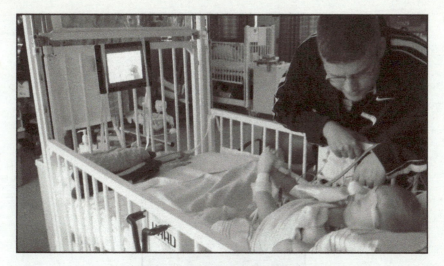

January 2015- Dad entertains Claire while we await a decision
on her transplant candidacy.

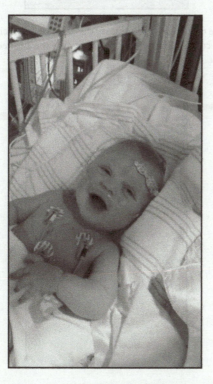

February 2015- One of the very few smiles we received
as we awaited Claire's hero heart.

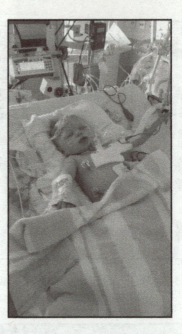

February 2015- Due to increased respiratory distress, Claire received a tracheostomy so the ventilator could allow her body to rest while she awaited her hero heart.

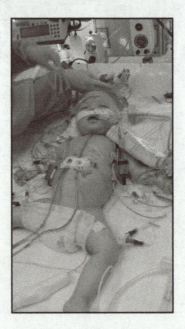

March 5, 2015- Only hours after her heart transplant, we were able to see our PINK baby.

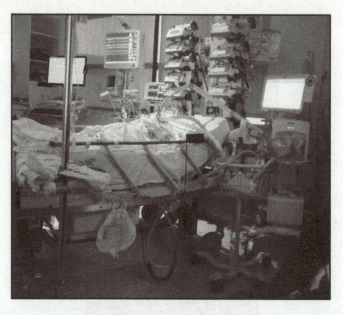

March 2015- Claire's CVICU room three days post-op from her heart transplant.

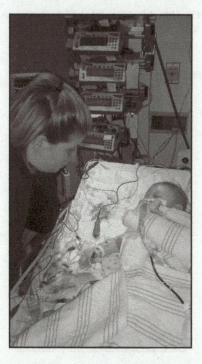

March 2015- Mom prays and sings over Claire after heart transplant.

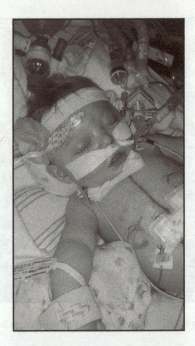

March 2015- Although still sedated, Claire begins to improve.

May 1, 2015- Claire smashes but does not eat any cake on her first birthday.

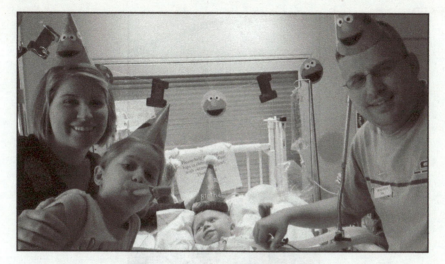

May 1, 2015- So very happy to celebrate Claire's first birthday, even in the hospital.

June 2015- Sister snuggles with Claire on the step-down floor.

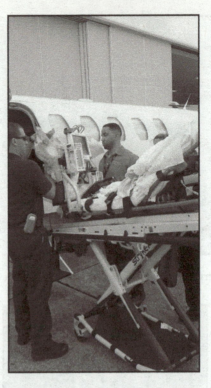

June 2015- Claire is transferred to her local hospital in Louisiana
to be near family as she continued her recovery.

July 4, 2015- Claire's first day home following her discharge
from her heart transplant.

September 2015- Claire enjoys watching TV and playing with her toys while sitting up in her highchair.

January 1, 2016- Chloe and Claire are looking forward to a happy new year!

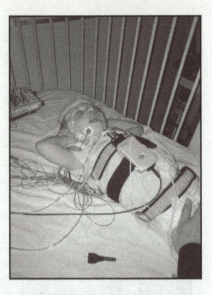

July 2016- Sleep study to determine if she can have her trach removed.

September 2016- Claire was admitted to the ICU overnight
to monitor her vitals after removing her trach. Claire passed!

December 2016- Mrs. Claus visited our home to bless the girls with holiday cheer.

January 2017- Claire receives physical therapy just before leaving for her autism evaluation.

March 2017- Our first family vacation! The girls pose with their gifts
after eating with Cinderella at Walt Disney World.

March 2017- Fairy God Mother caught Claire sleeping
and whispered a magic prayer in her ear.

April 2017- Claire and mom taking their afternoon naps in the hospital.

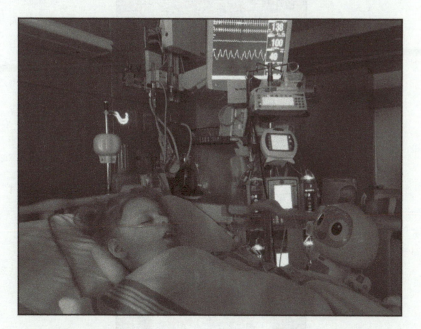

May 2017- Claire is admitted to CVICU unconscious and in septic shock
for a gram-negative bloodstream infection caused by the bacteria pseudomonas.

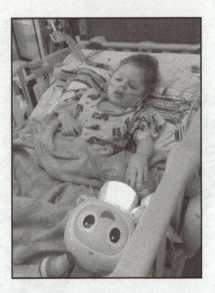

May 2017- Claire regains consciousness but very little strength—
only enough to press the button of her favorite toy.

June 2017- After one month of treatment for sepsis, Claire is discharged home.

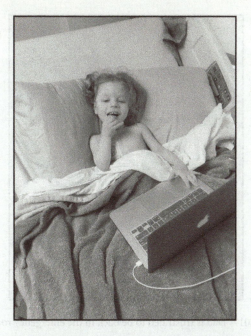

June 2017- Readmitted for dehydration, malnutrition, and fever. Claire helps mom with her work following her central line placement for IV nutrition.

July 2017- Home again and celebrating with sister.

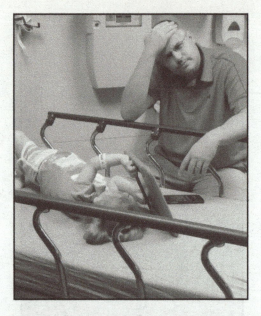

October 2017- Dad is frustrated to be back in the emergency room again.

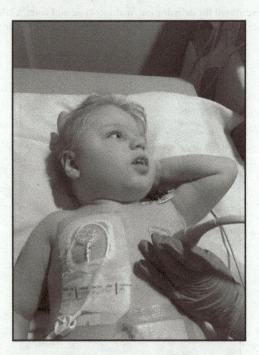

November 2017- Claire has gained weight and is much healthier due to her IV nutrition. She receives a clean bill of health at this cardiology visit.

February 2018- Claire experiences snow tubing at Gargoza Park.

February 2018- Skiing with the assistance of the National Abilities Center.

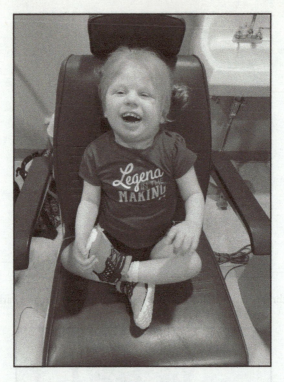

May 2018- Claire is all smiles during her ophthalmology appointment.

May 2018- Celebrating Mother's Day with this silly girl!

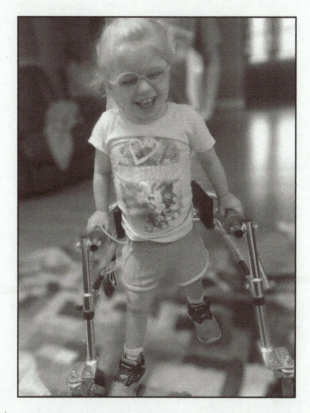

July 2018- Our big girl has come so far and continues to amaze us every day with her smile and unwavering strength. Praise God!

ACKNOWLEDGEMENTS

As I start to write this last portion, I feel I've come full circle. I started this book sharing my love for the song "For Good" from the musical *Wicked* and how it relates to my journey with Claire, specifically each time she is wheeled back into surgery or a sedated procedure. However, I can apply it to so many of you. I now know that each person I encounter throughout my life, both in good ways or bad, were brought to me for a reason—to learn from, to grow with, or for me to help. So it is with these thoughts in mind that I want to acknowledge those who've helped shape me for good.

Even if it may come across as corny, like an acceptance speech at an awards show, I would first like to thank *God* for not only continuing to strengthen me on this journey but for giving me the courage to follow the call to become a self-published author. Most nights I pray for God to work through me and give me the wisdom to distinguish between what is and isn't His path for me. No matter what, the process of writing this book has been cathartic, at minimum, and I pray it becomes a blessing to all who read it and to our family. Below are some other people in my life who deserve special recognition.

Kenny

I know your faith isn't as strong as mine, and that's okay. While I pray every night for your relationship with God to become stronger, I thank you for taking this leap of faith with me. You refused to read the book before it was published, so I hope you are pleased with your portrayal. I also hope you know how much I love you and value you as my partner in life. Oh, the places we've been and have left to go! If we continue to trust God and each other, we can make it through anything.

Chloe

Sweetheart, I pray you know how much I love you. Thank you for being my biggest cheerleader. You keep me in constant awe at the level of grace in which you handle nearly every situation. You are wise beyond your years, but the fact that you are still enjoying childhood with all that has been thrust upon you makes me incredibly happy. I also thank you for being an amazing big sister to Claire. I hope this book is one that you will share with your family and they with theirs and so on. I can't wait to see all the incredible things that await you in your life. You make me immensely proud.

Family

In an effort not to leave anyone out, I must acknowledge you all as a group. Each of you continue to play such an incredibly important role in our lives. I pray that each of you know just how much Kenny and I appreciate you. From helping with Claire, taking care of Chloe, keeping us fed, rallying support for fundraisers, bringing me chocolate, or keeping us in your prayers, we are blessed to have you in our lives. This journey would have crushed our family without your tremendous help and support. May God continue to bless you all!

Friends

Out of all the ways my mind has been blown in the last four years, you all, by far, have done it the most. To my "old faithful" friends, thank you all for immediately coming to our aid when we first received Claire's diagnosis. Though we may not have been in communication with each other in months or years, you all rallied to provide so much support and encouragement and continue to do so to this day. To all the friends I've made in the last four years I thank you, as well. Knowing that so many of you continue to keep our family in your thoughts and prayers continues to encourage me daily. I always say that I literally feel your prayers and positivity, and it makes all the difference!

Prayer Warriors

I could have included you all in the "friends" section because you truly are all my dear friends! Some of you have known me all my life and many of you only know me from social media as "Baby Claire's Mom." No matter how you know my family and me, if you have kept us in your prayers, you have played the most important part in our journey. On my worst days, when I was too overwhelmed or tired to pray, I always knew that we had a strong army of prayer warriors sending countless prayers to the heavens on our behalf. This always provided me comfort, and I have no doubt that you have shaped our journey "For Good." Thank you!

Claire's Medical Team

I have been intentionally very vague about where and from whom Claire has received treatment as not to sway people to and from providers because choosing specialists and caregivers for your child is an incredibly personal decision. However, I could not leave you all out of our acknowledgements. In my mind you are all a special part of our family, and always will be. Your jobs are not easy, and I know each of your participation in Claire's treatment has tested your limits (trust me—I KNOW). I hope Kenny and I have made it clear to you all how much we appreciate your hard work and love for our precious girl and our family. Hopefully, you all acknowledge the tremendous gifts you have in healing and comforting the sick and their families. You all should feel incredible pride in each day

Claire lives and every smile she smiles. Through your God-given gifts, YOU made it happen!

Heart Moms (and Daddies)

You are all the REAL DEAL! No comic book superhero team can hold a candle to a group of heart moms—NO WAY! The heart mom network is vast and a critical asset to any parent facing a new CHD diagnosis. From day one you were all there to offer encouragement, advice, and an ear to vent when that was what I needed. I can't even imagine what our journey would look like before social media linked us all together, because you have all supported our journey with your prayers and knowledge from the start. God bless all of you and your precious families!

You, the Reader

Thank you for purchasing this book and sticking with me until the end. Never in a million years would I have considered myself a writer. However, I felt a strong call to share Claire's story with as many people as possible. Over the years, so many people have told me that I should write a book. I never thought I could but when I started typing, the words and stories continued to flow. Thank you for being patient through my inexperienced writing. I hope you took some enjoyment in reading my work and that Claire's journey has helped you in a similar way it did me. Perspective is necessary in life. You may not be able to control what happens to you, but you can control how you respond to it. I hope these stories give you the perspective you need to respond appropriately—with prayer and thanksgiving for the good times and bad. All of your experiences shape who you are and the person you will become. Again, thank you!

To continue following Claire's Heart Journey, *visit*
www.facebook.com/clairebheart

ABOUT THE AUTHOR

Trista Brazan proudly resides in Southeast Louisiana. She graduated from Louisiana State University with a degree in Mass Communication, a concentration in Public Relations, and a minor in Political Science. After graduation she spent eight years building her career in non-profit and fundraising, advancing to the position of Executive Director in 2012. She left her career in 2015 to stay at home to raise her daughters, specifically her medically complex daughter Claire.

Trista had no aspirations of becoming an author; however, after the birth and subsequent medical journey with her daughter Claire, she was called to testify to how God can bring good—beauty and strength in the midst of much suffering.

Trista is happily married to her husband, Kenny, and mom to two beautiful daughters, Chloe and Claire. Despite life's constant struggles, Trista's family has learned to see God's hand in all situations and to have faith to believe He uses every situation to prosper us all.

To continue reading more of Trista's work, visit her blog at inchaotic-harmony.com where she shares how she survives life's chaos with music, Coke Zero, chocolate, and lots of FAITH.